brother earth

nature, God and ecology in time of crisis
brother earth
H. Paul Santmire
THOMAS NELSON INC.
New York Camden

Published in Camden, New Jersey, by Thomas Nelson Inc. and simultaneously in Don Mills, Ontario, by Thomas Nelson & Sons (Canada) Limited.

Library of Congress Catalog Card Number: 71-127072

Printed in the United States of America

To Laurel

Preface

The earth is in danger of destruction. Whether we lose our planetary home with a bang or with a whimper, by the population explosion driving us to mad Malthusian adventures or by massive pollution slowly poisoning us all, is finally a matter of indifference. The very future of our world is now in doubt.

The challenge of the contemporary ecological crisis is the springboard for this study. I am in full accord with the sentiments of historian Lynn White in his celebrated article, "The Historical Roots or our Ecological Crisis." "Since the roots of our trouble are so largely religious," White concludes, "the remedy must also be essentially religious, whether we call it that or not." [1] Today as never before we need an "ecological theology," [2] a theology which takes seriously the life of man in nature and the life of nature itself. Our time of crisis requires a religious vision which will teach us to say, in the depths of our being, "brother earth."

This book is intended as a step in that direction. The ensuing theological reflections are directed specifically to the large and disparate American Christian community. This community, in virtue of its size and its openness to new moral imperatives, has the potential of being a powerful force for ecological sanity in this country. But if the Christian church is to make a positive contribution in this regard, many things within the sphere of the church's own life and thought must be corrected and reformed. The church must begin to set its own house in order if it is to begin to respond adequately to the monstrous environmental problems of our time.

This book, furthermore, is a study in the theology of nature, *not* a study in "natural theology." It is concerned with the theological interpretation of the material-vital universe in which we live, and not directly concerned with the related problem of whether there is a natural or philosophical knowledge of God. Nor is it concerned with the pressing question of the meaningfulness and the validity of "God-language" in our time. The reader who is interested in these fundamental theological questions may profitably consult the recent work by Langdon Gilkey, *Naming the Whirlwind: The Renewal of God-Language*.[3] Gilkey deals at great length with a variety of important preliminary theological questions, which a study like the one before us can only presuppose.

The method the book follows is simple enough. Under the press of the contemporary situation, and drawing on the witness of the Bible and the theological tradition as both are received and celebrated in the worship of the contemporary church, the book tries to say something theological about nature that rings both forceful and true for those within the household of faith. At this point my own thinking has been shaped most explicitly by Dietrich Ritschl's balanced and incisive book, *Memory and Hope*. As Ritschl comments, "The *art of theology* consists in unfolding the divine reality in terms of human language in the full realization that human recognition must be imbedded in adoration. Theology unfolds in retrospect what has been recognized in faith and tested against biblical and other witness." [4] And, as Ritschl also maintains, "theological thinking is a circle which has no distinct and definable beginning. . . ."

Important as the proper theological method is, in other words, the proof of the method is in the doing, in the results. There is no single safe and reliable theological point of departure. Theology, like faith itself, is a venture, a risk. It has a context and materials to work with, but no self-evident master plan.

My reflections are dedicated with love and affection to my wife Laurel, who managed to read almost every word of my several drafts, and who joined with me in many discussions of those thinkers who were most on my mind as I wrote, Luther and Calvin, Thoreau and Marx, Tillich and Barth, and—always present in the background—the poets and prophets of biblical faith.

H. P. S.

Contents

brother earth

I. Nature and the American Heritage

Past the lawns of stately Mt. Vernon, the home of our nation's founding father, flows the stinking sewage-filled river Potomac. No one today sanely dares to swim in those waters. This ironic coincidence, a national landmark and a polluted river, symbolizes a fateful dilemma facing our society.

We venerate our past, so much of which is rooted in a profound sense for the land, the frontier, and the wilderness. "Such as we were we gave ourselves outright. . . . To the land vaguely realizing westward," Robert Frost said in his poem celebrating the inauguration of John F. Kennedy. Today we drink deeply of the world of nature around us, camping, hiking, sailing, and surfing whenever we can find the time. We are a nation which heads for the great outdoors on weekends or vacations, to relax and refresh ourselves.

But at the same time we find ourselves living in an immensely complex, highly industrialized urban society which again and again despoils our living space. Air unfit to breathe; water not suitable for drinking or even for swimming; open spaces no longer able to support wildlife; milk, fish, and other foodstuffs contaminated by pesticides–these are the legacy of our mass technocratic society.

Why is this so? How can we Americans so intensely adore and yet so violently abuse the land of our destiny? And how should we respond to this dilemma?

Many must make their voices heard if we are to answer these questions. We need the insight of the historian to help us understand how deeply the dilemma is ingrained in our national life.[1] We need the informed perspective of the natural scientist and the economist to help us see the extent to which we have polluted and over-populated nature, to suggest methods to curtail the pollution and the population, and to show us how to reclaim what we have despoiled. We need, as well, the passion of the conservationist and the preservationist. Without their voices to challenge our complacency, we may drift so far down the river of destruction that there will be no turning back.[2] We must also listen to our ecologists, our sensitive city planners and our humanistic philosophers, lest we thoughtlessly continue to build one vast blacktop jungle from sea to shining sea, with no unspoiled wilderness places, no fresh lakes, and few buildings designed to meet our primordial need to feel the pulse of nature where we live and work.[3] Above all, we need men of historic vision and political courage to speak in the houses of state and national government and through the mass media—men who recognize the drift of our society toward total pollution and over-population, who are willing to champion radical programs to change our course in defiance of intense counter-pressures mounted by special interest groups.

Along with the others, a theological voice must be raised. For many of the deepest roots of America's dilemma before nature are religious. Those roots must be unearthed and, where necessary, cast aside in favor of more vital theological values.[4] At the same time, a voice must be raised for the sake of the life of the Church itself, both with respect to its involvement in society and with regard to its involvement with its own tradition. How should the millions of Church members in this country understand and respond to the general American dilemma before nature, and how should they assess and react to the influence of that dilemma on the life of the Church? These essentially religious problems are the point of departure for this study.[5] Our destination will be a new theological interpretation of the material-vital universe in which we live and move and have our being.[6]

As we proceed we will be concerned with the *whole matrix of man's organic and physical existence.* We will not limit our purview to what Emerson referred to as "essences unchanged by man, space, the air, the river, the leaf."[7] For *wild nature* is just one aspect of the natural world. We will also be concerned with *cultivated nature* and with *fabricated nature,* that is, physical-vital reality as it has been changed, transformed, or even created by man.[8] We will be looking not only at the stand of virgin timber, the pristine lake, or the unmolested mountain peak, but at grain fields and flower gardens, skyscrapers and computers. We will be concerned with the whole physical-vital universe. If we were to choose to notice only wild nature, we would overlook both the breadth of the American dilemma and the comprehensiveness of the theological response required. The problem is not just that the heirs of George Washington can no longer swim in the Potomac. It is the much more fundamental problem that the life of man and the world of nature have been bifurcated. Properly the life of man, that is, "civilization," and the world of nature are *one* world. This is a theme we will return to again and again: man's very being is constituted not only by his relationship to God and to his fellow human creatures but by his relationship to the whole world of nature, by his life together with *all* of God's creatures, including those "creatures" fabricated by man himself.

It is of the essence of nature that it should offer a congenial living space, a home, to man. But civilization and nature have in fact been opposed to each other. The essential harmony of the created order has been disrupted. That is the major problem before us in this study. It is a problem which has been particularly evident in American history.

1. The Ethic of Adoration

American history is dominated by two apparently contradictory themes, Nature versus Civilization and Civilization versus Nature. This, observed Perry Miller, is the "obsessive American drama." [9] Neither act of this drama is peculiar to America as such. Each has deep roots extending back to the classical and biblical sources of Western culture. But the *obsessive* form of the drama, both as it pits nature against civilization and civilization against nature, is uniquely a product of the New World.

The historical roots of the first theme, Nature versus Civilization, are found at least as far back as Vergil, who celebrated the superior virtue and simplicity of the rustic life in his *Eclogues*. On the biblical side they are evident very early, sometimes strongly, in the wilderness motif of ancient Israel.[10] Later they appear in the lives of Christian monks and ascetics who left the corrupt life of civilization to find salvation in the wilderness. They also appear, in a unique way, in the person of St. Francis. The drama first began to be played with a profound sense of urgency, however, when urban industrialism began to alter not only the traditional patterns of daily life but to sap some of its fundamental biological resources, such as fresh air. The eighteenth century English poet, James Thompson, expressed a widespread dismay: [11]

> . . . Now from the town
> Buried in smoke, and sleep, and noisome damps,
> Oft let me wander o'er the dewy fields,
> Where freshness breathes, and dash the trembling drops. . . .

The drama took its "obsessive" form, finally, in America, where from the beginning the fundamental and overpowering natural reality was *the wilderness.* In a variety of ways, such writers as Henry David Thoreau, Ralph Waldo Emerson, James Fenimore Cooper, Francis Parkman and John Muir came to identify the vitality of American life with nature, and therefore to oppose it to the city, the railroad, and the steamboat.[12] This opposition was expressed most directly by Thoreau.

Thoreau himself was a complex thinker whose themes touch the reader's ear with symphonic force. But Thoreau's *legacy* was markedly simple and monotonal. Many if not most of his readers understood him to express an *ethic of adoration* toward nature. This theme struck a responsive chord among countless numbers of his countrymen. Positively, this ethic means that the individual should seek Deity, virtue, and vitality in nature, especially wild nature, and strive for personal purity and life for his soul through communion with nature. Negatively, the relationship to nature which this ethic occasions is so intense that little psychic energy is left for sustained intellectual and moral involvement in the practical social-political arena. The ethic of adoration fosters a general withdrawal from the organized city of man. That city is generally viewed as the godless, artificial arena of the mechanized, mindless, heartless mass-man. As Thoreau remarked, "The city does not *think* much. On any moral question, I would rather have the opinion of Boxboro than of Boston and New York put together." [13]

Two major themes of Thoreau's thought are of concern to us here. The first one definitely predominates over the second in his most renowned work *Walden* and in others like it, such as *Cape Cod.* In these writings we encounter the Thoreau who stands at the fount of the ethic of adoration, affirming that the wilderness is the town's source of life, a source which it cannot afford to forsake. In nature alone, not in the "pomp and parade" of the town, the individual may "walk with the Builder of the Universe." "Our village life," he writes, "would stagnate if it were not for the unexplored forests and meadows which surround it. . . . We need the tonic of wilderness. . . . We can never have enough of nature. We must be refreshed by the sight of inexhaustible vigor, vast and titanic features. . . ." He also sees nature as a teacher of humility and of a sense of finitude: "We need to witness our own limits transgressed," he observes, "and some pasturing freely where we never wander." Nature is a teacher of simplicity and virtue: "I am convinced, that if all men were to live as simply as I did [at Walden Pond], thieving and robbery would be unknown." Nature, then, was the existential substance of his life, and he tried to convince the reader that it should have the same import for all America. In his own experience, however, Thoreau continually felt hemmed in by "the dirty institutions" of men and by their pressures on him "to belong to their desperate odd fellow society." [14] This led him to look ever more passionately beyond civilization to the wilderness. He wistfully concludes his account of his journey to Cape Cod at its easternmost shore, at the sea, at the very edge of "Naked Nature": "A man may stand there and put all America behind him." [15]

That is the dominant theme in Thoreau's celebrated works on nature. The other theme comes to the fore especially in "Slavery in Massachusetts" and in his essays on John Brown. Here we see Thoreau the man of great moral passion, concerned with justice in society, even–for a moment–disenchanted with his love for mother nature.

For my own part, I commonly attend more to nature than to man, but any affecting human event may blind our eyes to natural objects. I was so absorbed in him as to be surprised whenever I detected the routine of the natural world surviving still, or met persons going about their affairs indifferent.[16]

Similarly, in "Slavery in Massachusetts" he asks about the meaning of "the beauty of nature when men are base." "Who can be serene," he muses, "in a country where both the rulers and the ruled are without principle?" "The remembrance of my country," he concludes, "spoils my walk." [17] So, he passionately and prophetically calls the state of Massachusetts to task for failing to free its own slaves while directing its political attention elsewhere. And he emphatically identifies himself with the ideal just state, while disassociating himself from the actual commonwealth in which he lived:

> Show me a free state, and a court truly of justice, and I will fight for them, if need be; but show me Massachusetts, and I refuse her my allegiance, and express contempt for her courts.[18]

Concretely, he identifies himself with the revolutionary action of John Brown: "It was his peculiar doctrine that a man has a perfect right to interfere by force with the slaveholder, in order to rescue the slave. I agree with him." [19]

These two themes, love for the wilderness and commitment to social justice, are also evident in the philosophy of Thoreau's Concord neighbor, Ralph Waldo Emerson, although in a considerably different way.[20] Temperamentally Emerson was not inclined to practice the rigorous rustic exercises commended in *Walden*. (He once refused to go on a hike with the naturalist John Muir, much to the latter's dismay.) Intellectually, Emerson approached nature more as a teacher for the Divine conscience in man than as a self-contained experience of raw and cleansing mystical communion. He has even been described as "a pious Platonist who went to nature for confirmation and illustration of his a priori ethical system." [21] But what Emerson apparently intended to say was not clearly heard by most of his readers, including many of his modern critics. His works were widely read as if they were but a more intellectual and more urbane version of Thoreau's *Walden*. For this confusion, Emerson himself was at least to some degree responsible, especially through the influence of his own famous paean to nature, the 1836 essay *Nature*.[22]

Emerson describes walking out into nature away from the institutions of man: "In the wilderness I find something more dear and connate than in streets or villages." He finds the enchantments of nature medicinal, healing: "Standing on bare ground–my head bathed by the blithe air, and uplifted into infinite space–all mean egotism vanishes. I become a transparent eyeball; I am nothing, I see all; the currents of the Universal Being circulate through me; I am part or parcel of God." [23] Like Thoreau, Emerson contrasts the charged experience of Deity in nature with the sterile ways and works of civilization. Sometimes the contrast is sharply etched: "These sunset clouds, these delicately emerging stars, with their private and ineffable glances, signify it [beauty] and proffer it. I am taught the poorness of our invention, the ugliness of towns and palaces. Art and luxury have early learned that they must work as enhancement and sequel to this original beauty." [24] Even if Emerson intended to present his own distinct moral message, his philosophy, like Thoreau's, had the effect of energizing the American ethic of adoration, opposing the healing wilderness to the stifling town.

This nineteenth-century ethic was intermingled, at least by implication, with a conservative social ideology. Adoration means being totally captivated by its object at the expense of other objects. So the obverse side of adoration was withdrawal from the town, sometimes even contempt for it. For the result was that lovers of nature consistently refused to participate regularly in movements for social, political, and economic betterment. Withdrawal and inaction finally became a tacit acceptance of the urban status quo.

This is vividly and paradoxically expressed in the writings of Thoreau. Despite his deep moral feeling and special hostility toward the institution of slavery, the thrust of his ethic is definitely away from sustained involvement in political affairs. He was personally inclined to disassociate himself from society: "Perhaps I am more than usually jealous with respect to my freedom," he wrote at one point; "I feel that my connection with and obligation to society are still very slight and transient." [25] This personal inclination found theoretical expression in a doctrinaire individualism and, concomitantly, a doctrinaire distrust of institutions. "The only obligation which I have a right to assume is to do at any time what I think right." [26]

The accent of Thoreau's articulated ethic falls, then, on the obligation to withdraw, rather than on the obligation to transform or overthrow: "It is not a man's duty, as a matter of course, to devote himself to the eradication of any, even the most enormous wrong. . . , but it is his duty, at least, to wash his hands of it, and, if he gives it no thought longer, not to give it practically his support." One's life thus becomes a "counter-friction to stop the machine by turning away from it." So, quite consistently, this enemy of slavery advises the abolitionists to "withdraw their support, both in person and property, from the government of Massachusetts," and not to worry about winning votes.[27] Thoreau even held that institutions *in themselves* are corrupt, not just that corrupt men use institutions corruptly: "In short, as a snow-drift is formed where there is a lull in the wind, so, one would say, where there is a lull in the truth, can institutions spring up." [28]

Which is the real Thoreau? The passionate critic of slavery or the radical anti-institutional individualist? We can only say that the real Thoreau is both, that there is a tension in his life and thought which he himself did not resolve.[29] The paradox, then, is this: on the one hand, an occasional but deep expression of hostility toward social injustice; on the other hand, a continually and passionately expressed morality of withdrawal from institutions in the name of nature.[30]

Thoreau's thought was an unstable compound that tended to disintegrate in the hands of less sensitive and less gifted followers. And when it did come apart, it was the passion for social justice that tended to be forgotten. The articulated ethic of adoration remained, with all its socially reactionary implications: God is in the vital wilderness, not with the effete community of men, and moral responsibility, accordingly, means to retreat from "the dirty institutions of men" and go to nature. If society is corrupt, leave it be; forsake it for the sake of your own moral purity, which can then be undergirded by the original virginity and fecundity of nature. Passionate moral sentiments against slavery fall to the wayside, and nature is more and more rigorously set over against civilization.

Although he himself was a concerned student of the political life of his time and although in other writings he stressed a communal moral responsibility, the ethic of adoration expressed in Emerson's *Nature* has similarly conservative social implications.[31] And a conservative ideology also flows from a whole host of lesser American writers who devoted themselves to nature. Many anthologies of popular poetry, for example, especially near the turn of the century, included selections like this one:

> I have come back to the city,
> With its clang and its screech and its din;
> Its halls are filled with madness
> And its eyes are blind with sin.
> I think of the peaks white-crested,
> And the sage on the sweeping plain,
> And the vastness, and silence,
> And the whisper of God again.

I will go back to the mountains,
    Back to the prairies I've trod;
Some day I shall stand in silence
    And speak once more with my God.[32]

The piety here is superficial compared to Thoreau's and the style is pedestrian compared to Emerson's, but the thrust is plain: God is not with men in the city, but with the individual alone in nature; virtue and vitality are not in the town, but in the wilderness. And this means, clearly, that it is morally permissible, even obligatory, to leave the city behind to stew in its own sin, perhaps waiting for the day when it will collapse because of its own decadence.

This message came through, sometimes clearly, sometimes more by implication, in the writings and speeches by many of America's early conservationists, particularly in the second half of the nineteenth century. Perhaps the most forceful and influential member of this group was the naturalist John Muir. He has rightly been called the publicizer of the wilderness of America.[33] Although Muir only restated aspects of the ethic of Thoreau, his works achieved a popularity Thoreau's had never known. His books were minor best sellers, and the foremost periodicals of the day bid for his articles.[34] Muir spent most of his life alone in the wilderness, and he scorned the city. He was at home only in the "hospitable Godful wilderness,"[35] where Divine balm for a wounded, decadent society could be found. "If you are traveling for health," he advised, "play truant to doctors and friends, fill your pocket with biscuits, and hide in the hills of the Hollow, lave in its waters, tan in its golds, bask in its flower-shine, and your baptisms will make you a new creature indeed. Or, choked in the sediments of society, so tired of the world, here will your hard doubts disappear, your carnal incrustations melt off, and your soul breathe deep and free in God's shoreless atmosphere of beauty and love."[36]

Although Muir fought tenaciously for national parks and to that extent was a participant in political life, his goal was to draw the hearts of his fellow citizens away from the city to the wilds. As he wrote concerning the national parks, "The tendency nowadays to wander in wildernesses is delightful to see. Thousands of tired, nerve-shaken, over-civilized people are beginning to find out that going to the mountains is going home; that wilderness is a necessity; and that mountain parks and reservations are useful not only as fountains of timber and irrigating rivers, but as fountains of life."[37] His own heart was where he wanted the nation's to be, not with the "clocks, almanacs, orders, duties, etc." of urban routine, not with the "lowland care and dust and din, where Nature is covered and her voice smothered," but with "the freedom and glory of God's wilderness."[38] There he saw "life at work everywhere, obliterating all memory of the confusion of man."[39] The ethic he lived was the gospel he proclaimed across the land.

Not always did the ethic of adoration entail such radical hostility toward urban civilization as it did for disciples of Thoreau like Muir. Those who were more interested in cultivated than wild nature, hearkening back to Jeffersonian concerns, knew that in some measure, the welfare of the land depends on the well-being and wisdom of the town. Typical was one Liberty Hyde Bailey, born in 1858. Bailey, a professor of horticulture well-known in the early decades of this century, wrote books with such titles as *The Outlook to Nature, The Nature-Study Idea, The Country Life Movement, The Holy Earth,* and a volume of nature poetry, *Wind and Weather.*

He also wrote a response to the political discussion arising out of World War I, *What is Democracy?,* as well as dozens of books on agriculture, horticulture, forestry and nature-lore. He was such a prominent figure in New York State that his name was once seriously mentioned in the press as a candidate for governor, and once he served on a presidential commission.

Bailey was interested both in securing the stability and the quality of life on the farm, and in conveying to the city dweller the benefits of a life close to nature. But along the way he was able to appreciate a number of positive virtues in the life of the city-dweller.[40] He also took a positive attitude toward political institutions, defining democracy as a form of government not only for the individual but for the welfare and development of all individuals.[41] Behind all this lay his conviction that the gospel of nature encourages social reform: "If nature is the norm, then the necessity for correcting and ammending the abuses that accompany civilization becomes badly apparent by very contrast."

Except for his 1918 book on democracy, however, Bailey did not usually go substantially farther than the expression of belief in nature as an impetus and a norm for social reform. Generally speaking, he simply was not concerned to develop or support political and cultural programs for the betterment of urban life. This is not to fault an intensely busy man for not doing something he had no time to do. It is rather to describe a certain mind-set not uncommon in the circles of those passionately interested in cultivated nature. His support of the Country Life Movement is typical of his interests. This was a program designed to undergird life on the farm for the farmers. As it was conceived, it was not a program for society as a whole; the needs of the city did not come into the picture in any noticeable way.

More to the point, Bailey frequently painted an idyllic picture of the farm, contrasting it favorably with the town. "I preach the open country," he wrote, "because it is natural and without affectation." "I preach the steadiness of country life, its freedom from speculativeness and from great temptation to evil doing." With several generations of American educators, moreover, he agreed that wild or cultivated nature is the best context for formal training for the young in truth and virtue: "Not the noise and glare and rush of inane city streets, but the majestic calm and beauty of the face of nature is the proper place for the spiritual nurture of young men and maidens during the few years devoted to higher education." "I am conscious that there is no soil in the city, but only dirt; the ground must be covered until it is blotted out." He was convinced that all men keep young and true by knowing nature. In this spirit he cited one of the "New Sayings of Jesus": "Raise the stone, and there thou shalt find me; cleave the wood, and there I am." Cultivated and wild nature, for Bailey, was the very reality of God and the fount of Divine gifts. "I preach the things that we did not make," he explained, "for we are all idolaters–the things of our hands we worship. I preach . . . the sky in rain and sun; the bird on its nest. . . , the smell of the ground; the sweet wind. . . . Wisdom flows from these as it can never flow from libraries and laboratories." [42]

If in theory Bailey's efforts were more moderate than the anti-urban tradition of Thoreau and Muir, practically they carried the same implications. And Bailey seems to have exemplified the mind-set of more than a few rural based academicians. The emphasis in his life and in his thought was almost exclusive devotion to the problems of the farm and to the idyllizing of cultivated and wild nature. He did not have an integrated view of society. The city did not figure substantively either in his daily work or in his reflection. The city was there, and occasionally it was noticed. But Bailey fundamentally dealt with one world only, the world of rural America.[43] That kind of practical emphasis could only lend further impetus, however subtle, to the already influential American ethic of adoration toward nature.

The kind of message that Bailey represented found some of its most passionate defenders among the leaders of America's churches. A student of the nineteenth-century American Church, Robert Cross, states that "almost every American churchman, in considering the problems of the city, contrasted them with the pastoral harmonies of rural culture." [44] Cross points especially to the writings of John Lancaster Spalding, a parish priest in New York City in the 1870's, who extolled the virtue of the farmer:

> He stands, like a portion of nature, permanent and changeless, the firm foundation to the whole social fabric. The lawyer, the doctor, and the preacher are the ministers of disease. They are nourished by the sins and infirmities of man. They were not in Paradise—could never have been there. Man, the farmer, was there, and the minister of nature was the minister of health and the minister of God.

To this idyllic vocation and location Spalding frequently contrasts the dirt, the debauchery, the artificiality, the godlessness, and the inhuman mechanism of life in the city. Spalding's remedy for the drastic urban situation was to "colonize" city dwellers in the country! His prescriptions may have been extreme, but Spalding expressed many sentiments held by several decades of American church spokesmen. Most churchmen, the reformist Presbyterian sociologist Charles Stelzle complained in 1907, seemed disposed "to meet town conditions by an elaborate country church programme."

In retrospect, this obsessive nineteenth century American theme of Nature versus Civilization, this ethic of adoration, may perhaps best be seen as a general cultural phenomenon paralleling the several utopian religious movements of that century. These religious communities were predicated on an intense dissatisfaction with the socio-political status quo, but they did not bring their utopian visions to bear on society to effect social change or revolution, as utopian movements on the continent often did. Rather they withdrew from society. And many of them, thinking of themselves in images borrowed from the Old Testament, went out into the wilderness to establish their own private holy refuges. There they sought God, virtue, and vitality, leaving behind in the cities the devil, sin, and death. They were concerned to establish a pure and vital Zion in the wilderness rather than to improve the dank and noisome life of Boston, New York, or Chicago. In a word, the American passion for wild and cultivated nature in the nineteenth century and later was predicated more often than not on a flight from oppressive social realities. Thereby that American passion functioned as an unconscious if not conscious force which supported the status quo in the burgeoning industrial city of man.

2. The Ethic of Exploitation

The city of man *was* burgeoning. During the nineteenth century the combination of invention, immigration, and utilization of vast natural resources set loose economic forces which eventually were to bulldoze the virgin American land into striking new contours. The steam locomotive, in particular, became "a kind of national obsession." [45] The nation sang about it, made political speeches about it, and wrote countless articles about it. America confessed a new faith in words like these, from a magazine article on the Pacific Railroad: "And the Iron Horse, the earth-shaker, the fire-breather, which tramples down the hills, which outruns the laggard winds, which leaps over the rivers, which grinds the rocks to powder and breaks down the gates of the mountains, he too shall build an empire and an epic. Shall not solitudes and waste places cry for gladness at his coming?"[46] This was the second act of the obsessive American drama, an act that went on simultaneously with the first, but which reversed its terms. This is the theme Civilization versus Nature.

This theme is as old as the history of man. From his earliest beginnings man has contended with the forces of nature to keep himself alive and to enhance his style of life. Men have always been disposed to raid the resources of nature for their own purposes. But this understandable human habit was always constrained by the reality of nature itself. Nature could not be exhausted by the primitive plow or the Roman iron mine. Forests could be leveled, to be sure, and often were; such mighty stands as the biblical trees of Lebanon were hewn down long before modern times. Yet the process took years of arduous labor and the ecological balance could adjust itself somewhat as the human work progressed. But when the steam engine arrived, a new era was born, for America in particular. With this machine men could digest natural resources at an astounding rate. The ancient theme Civilization versus Nature thus began to take its obsessive modern form in the *ethic of exploitation.*

The way for this ethic was paved by a number of cultural and economic forces. Intellectually, the mechanical view of nature championed by Descartes and Newton and widely accepted by educated men in the nineteenth century was a powerful, if indirect, influence.[47] According to this view, nature is analogous to a machine; or in the more popular version, nature *is* a machine. Nature is composed of hard, irreducible particles which have no color or smell or taste. Such qualities are "secondary." That is, beauty and value in nature are in the eye of the beholder; in itself nature is valueless. God may be the supreme initiator of the world-machine, but little more, for nature runs itself by itself, by its own intrinsic forces. God, often likened to a watchmaker, remains "back there" at the temporal beginning of the world, or "up there" in a wholly transcendent heaven; he does not "meddle" with nature now. Man too is set apart from nature, at least in his spiritual aspects. For him, nature is "out there," the dead *res extensa,* perceived by his mind, which observes nature from a position of objective detachment. This concept of a self-sufficient, self-enclosed complex of purely physical forces acting on colorless, tasteless, and odorless particles of hard, dead matter is the mechanical view of nature popularly accepted in educated circles in the nineteenth century.

The way for the ethic of exploitation was also prepared by the earlier Puritan doctrine of the dominion of man over nature. The Puritans emphasized the Genesis text which depicts God commanding man to subdue the earth and to have dominion over all creatures. They also believed that they were called upon to show the fruits of their election by their works, and so to glorify God. This, in brief, is what Max Weber referred to as the Protestant Ethic. Generations of Americans were instructed by their churches that nature is man's proper sphere of lordship, given by God to use, by the sweat of his brow, in order to bring honor to the name of God.

From its earliest days, this Puritan doctrine tended to coalesce with what Weber called the spirit of Capitalism. Spokesmen for capitalism argued, after the fashion of Adam Smith, that the ideal social system is the one which allows individual entrepreneurs freedom to use and develop natural resources, guided chiefly by their own self-interest. While the Puritan used nature to glorify God by the fruitful exercise of his Divinely bestowed dominion, the capitalist used nature to enhance his own enterprise and so to fulfill what he considered to be his own Divinely ordained destiny. For both, then, the chief criterion for man's dealings with nature was *utility*. We can conveniently refer to this coalescing of the Puritan doctrine with the apology for capitalism as *the utilitarian view of nature.* This view depicts nature essentially as a realm defined by its openness to manipulation and exploitation.

It is evident how harmoniously Puritan and capitalistic utilitarianism fits with the mechanical view of nature. The nature that is valueless in itself and essentially open to human manipulation is also defined by its quantitative aspects. As Lewis Mumford has observed, "The power that was science [i.e., mechanistic Newtonian science] and the power that was money were, in the final analysis, the same kind of power; the power of abstraction, measurement, quantification." [48] And the power that was science and money together was stimulated by the power of religious motivation, the power of the Puritan's ingrained drive to manipulate the world he encountered, whether that be by study or development. Thus the mechanical view of nature born in the universities, the Puritan approach sustained by the Churches, and the capitalistic attitude of the ever-expanding class of entrepreneurs came together to pave the way for the ethic of exploitation.

Positively, the ethic of exploitation calls for overcoming the ancient enemies of mankind, natural disasters, disease, and, above all, hunger. It also prompts the building of a society with a level of economic productivity and distribution to undergird political institutions which, in turn, will ensure individual freedom and security. Poverty is the door to serfdom; remove the first, said the popular logic, and the second will disappear as well.

Positively, then, the ethic of exploitation was egalitarian, whereas the ethic of adoration was conservative. Similarly, the ethic of exploitation was progressive, predicated on a vision of a commonwealth yet to come, while the ethic of adoration generally was regressive, harking back to a peaceable kingdom that has been lost, or is in process of being lost, through the incursions of civilization. Deity, moreover, is near at hand in the affairs of men, according to the ethic of exploitation. "The Kingdom of God is within you" might be chosen as the key biblical text for this ethic. People were encouraged to work and to build, to show by their deeds that God is with them and so to glorify Him. No one was urged to go out to the hills and survey the glorious firmament in order to find God. On the contrary, He is with men in their work and in their struggle with the elements. Correspondingly, virtue and vitality were not located in the raw wilderness so much as in the context of challenges posed by the machine.

When the ethic of exploitation was articulated in the nineteenth century those positive, progressive elements usually came to the fore in the form of revived Enlightenment notions of reason and progress which had permeated the American consciousness in the eighteenth century. A good example is found in the argument of a 1831 article, "A Defense of Mechanism," written by a young Harvard-trained lawyer, Timothy Walker.[49] This essay, a well-written apology for technological progress, celebrates the work of the machine over against the work of nature: "Where she denied us rivers, mechanism has supplied them. Where she left our planet uncomfortably rough, Mechanism has applied the roller. Where her mountains have been found in the way, Mechanism has boldly levelled or cut through them." Then, referring directly to the socially conservative approach to nature which here has been called the ethic of adoration, Walker argues that the machine has worked to liberate the masses of men. He refers to the development of various labor-saving devices and looks forward to a time when "machines are to perform all the drudgery of man, while he is to look on in self-complacent ease." Such leisure, Walker believes, will liberate the mind. More than that, a machine technology combined with the resourcefulness of the emancipated intelligence will bring in its wake an economy of abundance. The life of leisure, ease, and rationality led by the ancient Greeks can one day be realized not only for the few—who in Greece had to depend on a slave economy—but for the many.

Interestingly, and perhaps paradoxically, the author of *Nature* was also captivated by such ideas.[50] Emerson had been fascinated as a youth by Bacon and Franklin, and he never lost his faith in the power of science for progress. As he looked at his own times, he saw the light of reason advancing everywhere, and with it the forces of technological progress. "Railroad iron is a magician's rod," he wrote, "in its power to evoke the sleeping energies of land and water." "Gentlemen," he once told a Boston audience, "the development of our American internal resources, the extension of the utmost of the commerical system, and the appearance of new moral causes which are to modify the State, are giving an aspect of greatness to the Future, which the imagination fears to open." Characteristically, however, Emerson believed that the growth of cities should be curtailed. And at this point he stood somewhat apart from many of his fellow proponents of industrial progress. Emerson said he would defend "whatever events shall go to disgust men with cities and infuse into them the passion for country life and country pleasures. . . ." Even while he celebrated the locomotive, his hope for achieving a meaningful and virtuous life for America still relied on the purity of nature as an inspiration for the spirit of man. Celebrating progress, he yet would not give up his belief in the therapy of cultivated and wild nature.

This highly praised ethic of exploitation also had its pervasively negative aspects, already apparent to some by the middle of the nineteenth century. A sense of foreboding, for example, pervades the novels of Cooper, who created Natty Bumppo, that simple, pure child of wild nature. "In his mingling of anxieties and exultations," Perry Miller observes, "Cooper is indeed the central interpreter of his period; even while glorifying the forest-born virtue of America, he had also portrayed the brutal Skinners in *The Spy* and the settlers in *The Pioneers* who wantonly slaughter Nature's pigeons." [51] This irony of American history was stated well by Irving Babbitt in 1930, looking back at the preceding century: "No age ever grew so ecstatic over natural beauty as the nineteenth century, at the same time no age ever did so much to deface nature." [52]

The American story of the exploitation of nature has been told many times.[53] Ambitious entrepreneurs, with the acquiescence of an indulgent public, stripped a large portion of the nation's land of its virgin timber and abundant wildlife, exhausted much of its soil, and pockmarked its surface in the quest for minerals. The result was a series of man-made natural disasters. The infamous dust-bowls became the negative symbol of a growing and self-sure young nation. The same mind-set held children in factories in the cities and gave thousands of urban workers only a modicum of genuine nourishment for their stomachs and little truly fresh air for their lungs. The policy of Manifest Destiny and a faith in progress brought a spoliation of the rich material and human resources of the nation, with debilitating, not to say disastrous, results.

Curiously, toward the end of the nineteenth century this capitalistic devastation of men, women, and children in the cities, and of resources in the wilderness was justified by appeals to—nature. This time, however, it was not the genteel nature extolled by an Emerson, but a newly discovered world of supposedly natural process—nature evolving by the principle of the survival of the fittest. The new ideology of many entrepreneurs was "Social Darwinism." Raw nature, with its forces of darkness as well as light, which Thoreau so idolized as he turned his back on the city in *Walden,* had now penetrated into the city in the form of a pernicious, pseudo-scientific, social dogma.

This therefore is the historical shape of the American dilemma: In the nineteenth century the traditional Western theme of Nature versus Civilization becomes obsessive, developing into the ethic of adoration, a passionate fixation on wild and, to a lesser extent, cultivated nature, along with a turning away from the incursions of the machine and from the politics of the city. During the same century the theme of Civilization versus Nature also becomes obsessive and develops into the ethic of exploitation, a commitment to dominate nature for the sake of "progress," accompanied by a usually unreflective but sometimes deliberate devastation of natural resources.

How could both of these attitudes thrive at the same time in the same country? We will consider this fascinating question in some concluding observations at the end of the next chapter.

II. Nature in the Contemporary Milieu

The child is father of the man. That proverb expresses a singular truth about America's history with nature.

Much that has happened in the last hundred years would have led one to expect the proverb to have been proved false. The vast western wilderness areas which so captivated the American mind are gone. The loosely knit land-bound society of independent small farmers has given way to an interdependent mobile nation of city dwellers and suburbanites united by instant communication from one side of the land to the other. Civilization has virtually swallowed up nature, or so it might appear. One would have expected, then, that the obsessive American drama with nature would at least have begun to play itself out. The age of the megalopolis seems to be qualitatively different from the age of the frontier.

But while an older American nation may differ profoundly from its nineteenth-century childhood, with regard to America's life with nature, things are much as they were in the nineteenth century. The obsession has left an indelible mark on the American unconscious.

Morton and Lucia White may be correct in concluding that "romantic antiurbanism cannot be regarded as a permanent fixture of the American mind," [1] but only insofar as they are referring to certain representatives of the post-Civil-War intelligentsia. In mass culture today, the ethic of adoration not only survives but thrives in the form of a romanticizing popular ideology, *the cult of the simple rustic life.*

I. The Cult of the Simple Rustic Life

The cult shows itself in a wide variety of little places, for example, in articles and poems in our daily papers. In the largest city in America, the nation's most prestigious newspaper, the New York *Times,* regularly carries short editorials celebrating the seasons of the year and innocent nature poems such as this one on "The Peace of Wild Things":

> When despair for the world grows in me
> and I wake in the night at the least sound
> in fear of what my life and my children's lives may be,
> I go and lie down where the wood drake
> rests in his beauty on the water, and the great heron feeds.
> I come into the peace of wild things
> who do not tax their lives with forethought
> of grief. I come into the presence of still water.
> And I feel above me the day-blind stars
> waiting with their light. For a time
> I rest in the grace of the world and am free.[2]

The cult also appears in the popular art of Norman Rockwell and the mass-produced prints of bland landscapes and seascapes, and, at a higher level of sophistication, in the increasingly popular works of the painter Andrew Wyeth. It is manifest, too, in the resolute dash of millions of vacationers to the country, the mountains, and the seashores—to get that natural, rugged suntanned look. An excerpt from an advertising supplement on Hawaii, appearing recently in a number of mainland Sunday newspapers, tells at least as much about the American public's ideals as it does about Hawaii: "Hawaii is a sensuous, pleasure-giving land of extraordinary versatility and warmth. She's the beautiful bronzed Polynesian people with flashing dark eyes and quick smiles, the great expanses of silver beach, the gentle, warm aquamarine sea. She's the sleek, tapered palms stretching gracefully into the warm sun, the fertile valleys of bright flowers, crystal waterfalls cascading down lava cliffs into deep cool places. . . ." The lead article of the supplement was appropriately entitled "Tripping Through Paradise."

The popular cult of the simple rustic life is evident as well in the exclusive attention given to the natural life in hundreds of smaller national magazines on camping, boating, fishing and hunting; in the journals of conservation groups; and in the widely circulated publications of the National Geographic Society. It suffuses our commercial advertising, which regularly pushes cigarettes, shaving cream, and automobiles by highlighting the rugged individualist in the rugged country, the mountain climber, the deep sea diver, the cowhand. Men are offered masculinity in nature as tough "Marlboro Men," and couples are offered rustic bliss with Salems. In a not dissimilar way the cult of the simple rustic life appears memorably in the immensely popular creations of Walt Disney and his firm. One sensitive critic has written of Disney: "He prefers animals before men. His good guys are either animals or men living in the jaws of nature, more kindly brutes than men—e.g., the seven dwarfs." Disney's world "is shot through with nostalgia for the happy time prior to man's corruption, to which we can return if we will be instructed by the natural laws of the land God gave us." [3] We can see the outline of the same cult in the activities of many youth organizations, the Cub and Boy Scouts, Girl Scouts, and Campfire Girls.

Perhaps the most striking aspect of this cult is that it is largely unarticulated. It is much more a presupposition of contemporary American life than a professed ideology. The Coopers and Parkmans and Thoreaus are no longer prominent, but vast numbers remain unconscious adherents of a watered-down version of their religion: the flight to wild nature, the rejection of urban life. This is not to suggest that the cult of the simple rustic life has no exponents. Indeed it has more than a few, but they generally are not writers of the stature of their nineteenth century forebears, and they are frequently in close rapport with the popular cult, hardly ever assuming the radical stance of a Thoreau over against the whole of society and its "dirty institutions."

Here is one sample, from the credo of the "countryman," Hal Borland, author of scores of books and articles on nature: "The fact is that every civilization has been at its strongest, in human terms at least, when it was in some stage of its pioneering phase; when man was out there building a civilized society at the near edge of a wilderness, dreaming not of a sweatless utopia but of accomplishment with his own thew and muscle. . . . Both civilization and culture must be rooted somewhere, and all roots grow best in the soil itself." [4] Stewart Udall makes much the same point in his widely read book on conservation, *The Quiet Crisis*.[5]

The cult of the simple rustic life, interestingly, is less evident in the lives of many children of the affluent masses. Although they have been nurtured by the message of Walt Disney and other like-minded molders of public imagination and by a style of life dramatized in romanticizing Old West television programs, they nevertheless seem to be able to attune themselves to the pulse of urban life much more closely than their parents do. This is evident in their rock music, their light shows, and their experimental films. It is also evident in their political concern, which surfaced dramatically in the campaign of Eugene McCarthy in 1968 ("clean for Gene"), continuing through the various anti-war mobilizations in intervening years and coming to a highpoint in the national student strikes in the spring of 1970. Whether these young activists are thereby embracing or protesting against contemporary *urban* life is another question, but at least they are not directly turning against it en masse as their affluent parents have done. Indeed, many of the activists seem to be most at home in places such as New York or San Francisco.

On the other hand, the lives of many other American young people reflect their parents' cult of the simple rustic life, occasionally in remarkable ways. In some cases the cult has been internalized, so that the youthful individual tries to escape from the distressing problems of contemporary urban life not by motoring to the country or the seashore or the country, but by "taking a trip" to an idealized inner world with the help of consciousness-expanding drugs. His goal, as this is sometimes articulated, is to "turn on, tune in, and drop out." He may long for a place among the hippies, where "flower power" is supreme, where the simple virtues are a reality. He also seeks his Walden. This quest may be undertaken with only a few friends, passing a "joint" around ritualistically (as they passed the Indian "peace-pipe" when they were kids), in this way realizing a simple natural community which the atomization and bureaucratization of technocratic society inhibits. Or the quest can be a massive communal "trip," such as the celebrated gathering at Woodstock in 1969, where thousands sat in the mud, turned on, and generally lived out the simple elementary life in nature.

In some sectors of the drug culture, a Dionysian, mystical element comes to the fore. In this respect the contemporary drug culture is closer to the 19th century ethic of adoration than to the present day cult of the simple rustic life.

The beards and the blue-jeans worn by students tell much

the same story, as does the almost universal appeal of the Peace Corps, that rugged, simple, and self-reliant life far away from Boston and New York. Many other students can properly be termed "alienated." Burdened by the weight of "the system" or "the machine," they often seek refuge in a lonely life "on the road." Close study of them by Kenneth Keniston shows that "as a group, the alienated are wanderers, walkers, and hitchhikers: when confronted with a major or even a minor problem they are likely to 'take off,' sometimes for a long midnight walk, sometimes for a few years. . . . It is as if they were seeking some consoling contact with objects and things, contact more immediate and embracing than afforded by daily experience, and as if this contact could nourish and refresh them." They frequently have fantasies of mystical fusion with the universe—one thinks here again of Emerson's likening himself in his mystical ecstacy to a transcendent eyeball. They manifest "the unconscious desire to lose all selfhood in some undifferentiated state with another or with nature, to be totally embraced and to be embraced totally." [7]

Somewhat more dramatically, an increasing number of young people, especially along the West Coast, are creating the traditional cult anew with their passion for surfing. The ideal surfer is a replica of the venerated noble savage of yesteryear, riding the waves boldly, living on the beach in utter simplicity, growing a beard, getting dark brown skin from the sun. "Let's go surfing," in the words of one apologist means, "Let's get away from all this. Let's get out of this smoggy, congested city. . . ." According to the cult, surfing reflects its origins among the noble brown-skinned Polynesians in their island paradise: "It [surfing] was an integral part of the lives of a people who lived close to nature, to the sea. Surfing lived deep within their nature philosophy, in their religion—within the way of life we call Hawaiian." [8]

The latest manifestation of the cult of the simple rustic life is the much celebrated commune movement. An estimated 2000 hippies have "renounced the comfortable life," according to a recent story, "and come out here to the Taos wilderness to live in comparative poverty." Similar communes have been established in the past few years across the country, especially in California. One thinks also of the growing number of much more sophisticated centers for sensitivity training and encounter groups. More often than not these centers, such as Esalen or the newly established institute, "Cumbres," in New Hampshire, are set way off from Civilization in the wildnerness, where effete city people may revitalize themselves close to the bosom of mother nature.

The contemporary prophet of this cult of the natural, especially for a growing number of young people today, is the author of *Love's Body,* Norman O. Brown. Living in wooded isolation in the hill country overlooking the Pacific at Santa Cruz, California, Brown celebrates what he calls "polymorphous perversity," the instinctual, non-repressed, spontaneous natural life of the body. Brown's dionysian naturalism is caustically opposed to today's technological society and to the political enterprise in general. For him, as he said in an interview in 1967, "the real fight is not the political fight, but to put an end to politics." In Brown's thought, nature is opposed to civilization in the most radical Thoreauvian way. Indeed, Brown has recently remarked that he particularly loves America insofar as this is the country that provides a climate in which it is possible "to think about what it would mean to bring an end to that nightmare which is history." Brown has created a new—post-Freudian—Walden.

In its intensity and sophistication, surely, Norman O. Brown's vision often dwarfs the prosaic, part-time natural religion practiced by a sizable portion of those Americans today, both young and old, who like to think of themselves living the rugged life in nature. Nevertheless Brown exemplifies many of the deeper ramifications of the popular cult of the simple rustic life, particularly its fundamental suspicion of politics and its accompanying opposition to meaningful political change.

The cult of the simple rustic life, like the nineteenth century religion of nature, brings with it an implicit–sometimes explicit –social irresponsibility. It would be too much to say that the contemporary cult has been consciously developed in order to divert public attention from the pressing urban problems of the day. Indeed, in some cases a commitment to serve urban society is in evidence. Still, there can be little doubt that the cult of the simple rustic life does reenforce a commitment to the status quo, especially in the ranks of the small town, suburban, and affluent urban citizenry. The vast sums expended on boating and camping, for example–think of those shiny "boat shows" and "camparinas" in the public auditoriums located in the midst of the decaying inner city–not to speak of the emotional investment, are diverted, at least in part, from support for low-income housing or establishing efficient mass-transportation systems. Consider also the popular devotion to leisure time in the forest and the mountains, particularly as that sometimes comes to a symbolic focus in conservation projects such as saving the California Redwoods. President Johnson, delivering his State of the Union Message in January 1968, mentioned such urban concerns as civil rights, fair housing, and equal opportunity employment, and there was no noticeable response by the listening Congress. He then indicated his interest in saving the Redwoods, and the whole Congress came alive with loud applause. Surely, no sensitive citizen would want to see the magnificent Redwood forests any more desecrated than they have been. But silence for the city and applause for the trees discloses some of the Congress's deeper feelings and, behind that, the deeper commitments of many whom it represents. Two years later in his State of the Union Message, President Nixon—apparently very much in touch with the majority mood of the nation—proclaimed that the "great question of the seventies" is the environmental question: "Shall we . . . begin to make reparations for the damage we have done to our air, to our land and to our water?" In the same speech the President hardly mentioned making reparations to our decaying and deprived cities and to minority groups, particularly the blacks, who live there.

The conservatism implicit in this stance—the social ills of the city can wait, while we seek to heal the world of nature—is reflected, as we might expect, by the alienated children of the Silent Majority. This relatively small but representative group of middle class students shows a sustained contempt for political involvement in general and urban involvement in particular. For them, the thing to do is to *drop out* of society. As Keniston has written of these alienated students, "One basic, though usually hidden premise of much of their thinking is the principle of implicit conservatism. In alienated fantasies, we have seen repeatedly that revolution ends in disaster for all concerned. The ideological corollary of this fantasy is that one should seek to change the world as little as possible, for no matter how numerous its present evils, they will be succeeded by other evils just as devastating if not more so." [9] On the other hand, as we have seen, this same group is as a general rule very much taken by a cult of the simple rustic life reminiscent of the nineteenth century ethic of adoration which also was essentially regressive, which depicted society as falling away from a pristine and virtuous life in nature.

The cult of the simple rustic life might be interpreted as a protest. Present day urban, technological society is full of a thousand jagged edges. This has been amply documented by such critics as Lewis Mumford and Herbert Marcuse and by the writers of works like *1984* and *Brave New World*. Yet if it is a protest, and that is by no means clear, in the last analysis it is an inarticulate, mostly unconscious, unconstructive, and therefore highly ineffective expression of discontent.

2. The Cult of Compulsive Manipulation

The other side of the cult of the simple rustic life—as the ethic of exploitation was the obverse side of the ethic of adoration—is the *cult of compulsive manipulation*.

Americans today venerate, perhaps as never before, what Paul Tillich called "technical reason," the cognitive faculty that calculates means for ends, which functions to "get the job done," as distinct from reflective reason which sets goals in the context of some larger structure of meaning. We Americans do not generally question why we should go to the moon; we leap to the decision and set thousands of technicians to work on the project. As Keniston has observed, " 'Competence,' 'know-how,' 'efficiency,' and 'expertise' are prominent national virtues; and though we may consciously acknowledge that these are at best instrumental qualities, we often unconsciously pursue them as independent goals." [10] We are prone to manipulate our environment without question. If we need a fast avenue from here to there, let it be built. If that superhighway throws thousands out of their homes and destroys landscapes and forest preserves, so be it. If we need, or think we need, chemical weapons to fight the next war, we will have them and let the overflow fall where it may. Once Americans have the expertise to get a job done, all it takes is a usually impulsive decision to begin, and the project will be underway. Americans today are compulsive manipulators of the first order.

This cult seems to have shaped the very centers of our personalities. Using the classical Freudian terminology Keniston refers to this as the "tyranny of the ego." Properly, the ego should be the integrating center of the personality, giving way to passion (the id) when that is appropriate, and to moral fervor (the superego) when that is appropriate. But in practice in our society today the ego manipulates much more than it serves the self. In particular, it habitually dominates the unconscious elements of personality and the vitalities of the body, almost to the point where they can no longer be seen in themselves; when they rise to the surface, as they inevitably do, they frequently do so in irrational, uncontrolled expressions of aggression. The tyranny of the ego produces the man who is "perfectly in control of himself," a man who rarely if ever consciously "let's himself go" spontaneously in sex, play, or fantasy.

We can see a parallel between the patterns of our society and the patterns of our personalities. The individual is constantly prone to manipulate his environment, while the conscious center of his personality, his ego, is constantly prone to manipulate his personality. To quote Keniston again: "In these terms, the virtues of our technological society require a dictatorship of the ego rather than a good government. The self-denying potential of the ego is minimized: Playfulness, fantasy, relaxation, creativity, feeling, and synthesis take second place to problem-solving, cognitive control, work, measurement, rationality, and analysis. The technological ego rarely relaxes its control over the rest of the psyche, rarely subordinates itself to other psychic interests or functions. Though its tyranny is seldom obvious, it is firm and unrelenting." [11]

This analysis is well illustrated by the popular television series "Mission Impossible," a technological corollary to the simple, rustic "Bonanza." "Mission Impossible" reflects the *cool* technocratic generation: men and women without feelings (except for a cool efficient smile now and then), without sex, without playfulness, and also without noticeable moral convictions. They simply accept their instructions from the voice on the tape recorder and then, with technical skill and ingenuity, get the job done, no matter what. The robot people of "Mission Impossible" reveal both the sociological and the psychological pathos of the cult of compulsive manipulation.

It can be no surprise, then, that we who habitually manipulate our world and our inmost selves without much reflection, continue to deplete and deface the resources and the beauty of our natural environment much as our nineteenth century forebears did. It is the old Manifest Destiny attitude toward nature clothed in cool technological garb. Our air, especially in places like New York City, Los Angeles, Detroit, and Gary may well be cancer-inducing, as cigarette smoke seems to be. Our milk and fish and hundreds of other foodstuffs are contaminated by DDT. Our water, almost everywhere in the nation, is in shorter supply and less drinkable. In 1956 Lake Erie was relatively clear and full of fish (the yearly catch of blue pike alone was some seven million pounds), but today the lake simmers with human waste and chemicals; it has virtually no fish left. Continent-long ribbons of cement with their omnipresent billboards, cover more and more of the nation's earth and cut away more and more of the nation's neighborhoods and wilderness areas. Our cities, as few need to be reminded today, are decaying: older buildings are blighted, newer "urban renewal projects" are often so insensitively built and inadequately cared for that few choose to live in them. Everywhere the refuse of planned obsolescence piles up. Each year Americans discard seven million autos, twenty million tons of paper, forty-eight billion cans, and twenty-eight billion bottles and jars, many of them in the form of indestructible plastics and aluminums. Contemporary technological-urban society is polluting the rooms of its own house, with little public effort to halt it. Even in some of our wilderness areas, the pollution piles up. From 1957 to 1963, for example, the Sierra Club's projects to pick up discarded cans and bottles from wilderness areas in the Sierra reported twenty-three and one-half tons removed! It was the former Mayor of Detroit who said that we may be known as the generation which went to the moon while standing knee-deep in garbage.

Conservationists, sometimes disregarded as "romantics," are now supported by a wide variety of unromantic, hard-headed natural scientists. The growing scientific consensus is that we in America are in danger of destroying our own natural foundations. "Mankind is living incredibly dangerously," one of them told a Congressional committee some time ago. "We are living with and disturbing, disrupting, and attempting to manage the earth's surface," he continued, "without understanding the effects of our actions." [12] The American Association for the Advancement of Science issued similar warnings several years ago, and repeated them again at the end of 1969.

Compulsive manipulation, it hardly needs to be added, is also an institutional phenomenon today, particularly through the powerful agency of modern technology, when the latter is coupled with the manipulative mind-set. To varying degrees, the white collar worker in the large firm, the suburban housewife, the young man of draft age, the welfare mother, the unemployed black in the ghetto, the Vietnamese or Laotian living in a "free fire zone," and many others find their lives dominated directly or indirectly by gigantic computerized bureaucracies. Whole masses of people today are regimented, sometimes brutally, sometimes very subtly, by powerful institutional forces beyond their control. The cult of compulsive manipulation is all-pervasive. Its domain is social and political as well as environmental and psychological.

Like the cult of the simple rustic life, however, the cult of compulsive manipulation is largely without conscious articulation, and that makes it all the more difficult for the public to identify and to correct. It is much more a style of life than a philosophy of life. Few people today, surely, would be willing to defend the tyranny of the ego or the pollution of nature. On the other hand, few people are prepared to ask, for example, whether the detergent they regularly use is the indestructible variety that pollutes our streams. In the main, the cult of manipulation is an unconscious habit, still buttressed by the three pervasive cultural forces, the mechanical view of nature, the Protestant doctrine of man's God-given dominion over nature, and the still venerated ideology of the entrepreneur. The last two need no comment at this point, since they function in the contemporary milieu much as they did in the nineteenth century, as ideological reenforcements for an already established pattern of life. But the fact that the first, the mechanical view of nature, also functions this way is something of a surprise.

Contemporary physics has criticized and passed beyond the mechanical view of nature. One would think that that development would have influenced our approach to nature. But the impact of contemporary physics, which deals of course with unobservable sub-atomic particles, has not been felt in the context of daily experience. The mechanical view is still adhered to by educated people in America today. If he does think reflectively about nature, the engineer or the research technician employed by the large company or by government is much more likely to think of nature in mechanical terms than any other way. That is the mode of thought in which he has been trained and that is the mode of thought which is most congenial to "getting the job done," which is what his company or the government wants him to do. In such ways, adherence to the mechanical view of nature continues to be a form of support for the cult of compulsive manipulation.

So nature, a perpetual dilemma for American society, remains a problem today. The American mind still suffers from a kind of schizophrenia: we continue both to worship nature and to exploit it, perhaps not so enthusiastically as our nineteenth century predecessors, but just as relentlessly. Now, as then, there are individual exceptions to the rule. Not everyone is a true believer in the cult of the simple rustic life, not everyone participates daily in the American liturgy of compulsive manipulation. But as far as our relationship to nature is concerned, both cults, like the ethics of adoration and exploitation a century ago, continue to be the dominant colors in the fabric of American society.

3. The American Dilemma

How can both attitudes exist in the same culture in such pervasive ways? Logically, the cult of the simple rustic life and the cult of compulsive manipulation would seem to be contradictory. Recalling the contours of the nineteenth century ethics of adoration and exploitation, we arrive at the same conclusion about them: The American approach to nature apparently has consistently been a contradiction in terms.

To explain how this apparent contradiction can be sustained, we might observe that in the nineteenth century the two conflicting attitudes toward nature were characteristic of *two relatively distinct groups:* on the one hand, the nature philosophers and nature lovers who were fearful of the machine, and certain older aristocratic segments of society; on the other hand, the growing group of city-based entrepreneurs, an urban proletariat work force, and many hardy frontiersmen inclined to view the nature not as a friend but an enemy, not as a landscape but as a life-and-death challenge. The two ethics were thus held, generally speaking, by two different social groups.

The explanation for the contradiction today might be somewhat different, since the adherents of the cult of the simple rustic life are mainly suburbanites and affluent urbanites actively involved in the mainstream economic and academic processes of our society. They are thereby priests of *both* the cult of the simple rustic life and the cult of compulsive manipulation. How can the same individual have two religions? To answer this question we could say that both cults are largely unarticulated, and that for this reason both lend themselves to easy *compartmentalization*. The suburbanite or the affluent urbanite works in the city; he dreams of the country. He works on a sonic-boom producing SST, perhaps; he lives in a "ranch house." His life has two foci, and he does not feel compelled, nor is he in fact compelled, to relate the two reflectively. Here, then, it is not a case of two segments of society holding contradictory views, but of a species of schizophrenia: one unreflective, compartmentalized mind-set. A revealing example of the success of that compartmentalization is the state of our national parks, to which prosperous thousands flee for spiritual refreshment during the summer, and over which they litter tons of paper and soft-drink cans as they drive through.

Does the contemporary suburbanite and affluent urbanite not know that he is, and somehow seems to need to be, the priest of two cults? Is he not aware, at some level of his personality, of his compartmentalized approach to his natural environment? Perhaps there is a deeper explanation that religious insight may suggest.

From a theological perspective, the American schizophrenia appears to have its deepest roots in *a failure to meet the challenge of historical existence*. Man is through and through a historical creature. He can look forward to new developments as he remembers his past. He is given freedom by God to shape his life self-consciously and to be a voluntary and responsible participant in the Universal Divine History with all things. Man, in other words, is not tied inextricably to the cycles and the cyclic processes of nature. He has his life in nature, but he transcends it in personal, historical freedom before God.[13]

But history brings with it anxieties and responsibilities which can weigh so heavily on the life of man that he is tempted to relinquish his historical destiny for something less, a purely natural destiny. Faced with an open future, conscious of his own transcendence of nature, man can be threatened by severe existential anxiety about his destiny and his own final goal. Faced with the continuing Divine call to moral responsibility, moreover, and aware of his own failures, the threat of the future and the attendant anxieties can be further intensified. In this way historical existence can become so unbearable that man turns away from history to find "worldly security" (in Bultmann's words) in the morally undemanding stability of nature.

The challenge of historical existence emerged in the life of ancient Israel in a way which illuminates our present situation. The biblical God, Yahweh, was the Lord of history, the ruler of the future and of social change.[14] In contrast, the gods of Israel's neighboring peoples were nature gods,[15] entwined with the recurring cycles of the seasons. Hence they were gods of stability and recurrence, both natural and civil. With regard to social morality, Yahweh was a God of social justice while the deities of the nations, the Baalim, were gods of the status quo.

This biblical perception of God and history, this affirmation of historical existence, produced anxiety in the minds and hearts of those who adhered to it: a whole people was called to stake its life on an uncertain Future, the coming Kingdom of God, which required moral obedience and action leading to social justice. The anxiety is reflected, for example, by the Deuteronomic historian who notes how the people "would not go up," how they "murmured in their tents, and said, 'Because the Lord hated us he has brought us forth out of the land of Egypt, to give us into the hand of the Amorites to destroy us." (Deut. 1:27) The people were not eager to accept the challenge of leaving the secure status quo and venturing out into an unknown and hazardous future. That is one side of the challenge of historical existence. The life in history brings anxiety; the life in nature, in contrast, is at least a pattern of orderly events and therefore is not so fearful. And, as the challenge of the first mounts, the pull of the second increases too.

The other side of the challenge is the experiential failure of the historical people to be fully obedient to the claims of the coming Kingdom of God which requires executing justice one with another, not oppressing the alien, the fatherless, or the widow, not shedding innocent blood (Jer. 7:5). The people of Israel were, in fact, disobedient. As Hosea depicts the history of Israel, the fabric of pure Yahwism was torn by economic self-seeking among the people: "It was I who knew you in the wilderness, in the land of drought; but when they had fed to the full, they were filled, and their heart was lifted up; therefore they forgot me" (Hos. 13:5-6). The fabric was also torn by political disobedience: "They made kings, but not through me. . . . For Israel has forgotten his Maker, and built palaces; and Judah has multiplied fortified cities" (Hos. 8:4, 14). So, in Hosea's eyes, due to both economic and political aggrandizement, the underlying socio-religious foundations of Israelite society had begun to crumble.

In such a context, with anxiety before the future and disintegration of the essential moral response to Yahweh, the gods of the surrounding peoples in Canaan made inroads into

Israelite life. Faced with uncertainty and fragmentation, many in the nation began to be attracted to the predictable stability offered by the gods of nature. The very wealthy, concerned to hold on to their riches, had special reason to devote themselves to the Baalim and to encourage the masses to do so as well. The prophets continually recalled the people to historical faithfulness to the God of history against the alluring and non-demanding stability of alien worship. The gods of nature had their appeal both as an *escape* from the rigors of historical existence and as a *refuge,* for poor and wealthy alike (although for different reasons), in a time of socio-religious fragmentation.

The people of the New World, many centuries later, came to experience the challenge of historical existence with great intensity. The American historical consciousness was shaped first by the "Exodus" from the Old World to the New, then by the continuing "Errand into the Wilderness," which Perry Miller has described. The Enlightenment faith in progress—a secular distortion of the biblical understanding of history—reenforced this historical consciousness.

A belief in progress presupposes a historical sense, looking forward to *the new* and to change for the better in contrast to recurring natural cycles. In this American context, as in the life of ancient Israel, there was both anxiety before an uncertain future and a sense that the nation had failed, or was failing, to live up to its promise. With the additional achievement of a certain level of prosperity, the wealthy tended to desire a more stable order. The anxiety and sense of failure, together with the desire to protect a given economic order, were perhaps most dramatically evident in the Civil War and in the profound impact it had on the nation. During that period it was not clear whether that nation would even survive, much less whether it would be a land of justice for all men or which economic matrix would dominate, the agrarian or the industrial. Faced with the Civil War and with many similar nineteenth-century upheavals of which that War was more or less the symbolic apex, the nation was understandably attracted to nature.[16] With her history being shaken to its foundations, the predictableness and the stability and—here we meet the peculiarly American motif—*the purity* of nature were profoundly attractive.

In our own time we can see a similar anxiety operative in the life-style of our "alienated students." For many of them the horrendously uncertain future is symbolized by the prospect of atomic holocaust. They also see our society as having failed radically to live up to its promise of justice for all men. So they drop out, take a trip, wander across the nation, join in wilderness communes, reinterpreting the cult of the simple rustic life they learned from their affluent parents. For those in whom the challenge of historical existence is felt most acutely the allure of the gods of nature is felt with corresponding power.

On the other side of the generational dividing line today, in the ranks of the older so-called Silent Majority, we now hear simultaneous cries for "law and order" and pleas to pay "reparations to nature." This conjunction of slogans is only the most blatant verbal expression of a widespread refusal on the part of middle-class America to meet the challenge of historical existence. The many-faceted, pervasive cult of the simple rustic life seems to function in alliance with an underlying commitment to the political status quo. But the political status quo is disintegrating in our time, and this is a serious threat to those entrenched in power. So they focus their own attention even more on (the stability of) nature, and hope to entice others with nature too. Whereas many of their children are dropping out of a society they detest, and in turn are going to nature as an escape, these elders cherish the received society and turn to nature, it seems, in the hope that somehow in this way society will disintegrate no further.

Nature thus has functioned in nineteenth and in twentieth

century America, as in ancient Israel, both as an escape for those who have despaired over the society's failure to give justice to all, and a refuge for those who have "made it" and fear further social change. The ethic of adoration and the cult of the simple rustic life have functioned as an existential rejection of history, in the full theological sense of that word.

The other American theme, Civilization versus Nature, in both its nineteenth and twentieth century forms, has functioned in a similar way. Man's transcendence of nature was pushed to an extreme in the modern industrial West. The freedom of historical existence was employed *against* nature. Rather than accept a balanced and harmonious interrelation of nature and history, those who had benefited most from the birth of a thoroughgoing historical consciousness made war on nature. Nature had been demythologized, the power of Baal undercut; but to the winner went the spoils. Nature became a mere object for exploitation and compulsive manipulation, particularly in America.

We can see existential forces at work here which are very much like the ones behind the flight to wild and cultivated nature: anxiety before an uncertain future, and a quest for stability in a time of social fragmentation. Rather than flee to the wilderness or the farm, as a way of finding worldly security before the challenge of historical existence, men sought to amass trophies from their struggle with nature. They turned to Mammon instead of Baal for security. He who garnered the most wealth was he who could feel most secure. He had his "life insurance" in his material goods. They protected him from anxiety and gave him the power he needed to allow him to hold on to his status in society when that was challenged, directly or indirectly by the dispossessed. This was and is the existential basis for the ethic of exploitation and the cult of compulsive manipulation; both are manifestations of the same underlying tendency to seek worldly security by domination of nature, turning away from the insecurity of an open future and the demand for social justice. The escape to nature in this context, to be sure, took the form of aggression rather than adoration, but the existential precondition remained the same in both instances: the desire to flee history for a refuge in the stability offered by nature.

Nothing comparable to modern exploitation of nature was known in biblical times. Exploitation and compulsive manipulation were simply not possible on so vast a scale in preindustrial, pre-technocratic societies. Still, the power of Mammon was certainly acknowledged and challenged in the Bible for what is was, for example by the prophet Amos:

> Therefore because you trample upon the poor and take from him exactions of wheat, you have built houses of hewn stone, but you shall not dwell in them; you have planted pleasant vineyards, but you shall not drink their wine (Amos 5:11).

In the Sermon on the Mount Jesus also questioned men's priorities:

> Therefore I tell you, do not be anxious about your life, what you shall eat or what you shall drink, nor about your body, what you shall put on. Is not life more than food, and the body more than clothing? But seek first [God's] Kingdom and his righteousness, and all these things shall be yours as well (Mt. 6:25, 33).

The biblical writers saw the compulsive amassing of wealth as a refusal to accept responsibility for the righteous claims made by God on the lives of men. The difference between biblical and modern times lies not in the kind of response men made to the challenge of historical existence, but in a *quantitative* factor. In contrast to biblical times, the results of modern allegiance to Mammon have been an immense devastation of nature.

With a theological perspective based on biblical insights we can begin to understand why middle class America in the last two centuries has been able to shift back and forth between adoration and exploitation of nature, from the cult of the simple rustic life to the cult of compulsive manipulation. The apparent contradiction is actually no contradiction once the underlying existential reality is uncovered. The contemporary suburbanite can be enamored by the simple rustic life and a habitual participant in compulsive manipulation because both cults have the same foundation in a rejection of authentic life in history for the sake of worldly security. Adoring nature and exploiting nature are two sides of one coin used to buy release from the challenge of historical existence.

If the obsessive American drama is in some sense a replaying of the biblical drama of men turning from Yahweh to follow either Baal or Mammon, then the Bible may provide some clues for resolving our present dilemma. Indeed, the dilemma Nature versus Civilization and Civilization versus Nature *is* resolved in the Bible, particularly by the prophetic tradition. Here the challenge of historical existence is recognized and accepted, self-consciously and passionately, while at the same time, nature and civilization are understood to be in harmony. Each is allotted its own place, yet never fundamentally in opposition to the other. For the biblical tradition, civilization and nature are distinguishable, but they are *one* world. They are brothers, not enemies.

III. Nature and the Life of the Church

The decade of the seventies has been widely called the Age of Ecology. In the first months of the new decade national publications joined the crusade, and many divergent national groups took up the banner, liberals and conservatives, farmers and suburbanites, the League of Women Voters and a number of "radical" student groups. The President himself placed his prestige and power at the head of the column in his 1970 State of the Union message, telling the nation that the time has come for us to "make our peace with nature." Ecological problems, such as the population explosion, exhaustion of national resources, and pollution, are in the forefront.

Church leaders and laymen across the country have also begun to identify themselves with the concerns of the Age of Ecology.[1] But as the Church has been responding to the environmental crisis (appropriately if somewhat slowly) little attention has been given to the role that nature plays *within* the Church. It has been assumed almost without question that the problem is "out there," in the world, but not in the inner life of the Church. But the problem has roots and ramifications there as well as within society as a whole. Indeed, horrendous as the national and international ecological crisis is today, the Church will be well advised to consider first the situation inside its own walls. For it seems clear that the

Church will not be able to make a significant contribution to society in this regard until it has at least begun to put its own house in order.

1. The Simple Rustic Life and the Church's Political Involvement

Within the Church we find symptoms of the familiar American schizophrenia, but with certain idiosyncratic characteristics. In American culture generally, the schizophrenia is not only subtly evident but articulated at least to some degree. The experience of desiring to flee to wild or cultivated nature and, at the same time, in actuality, living in a society which markedly exploits the natural world, has a small but audible verbal accompaniment. The self-styled naturalists advocate the flight to nature, while the prophets of the "free enterprise system" defend the dominion of man over nature and its use for man's purposes.

In the life of the American church, however, the same contrast is present, but neither viewpoint has theological spokesmen. The result is that virtually no one openly defends the flight to nature. And by default if not by conscious intention, many support the exploitative utilitarian approach.

The publicly professed theology of the contemporary American church has little or no place for self-conscious advocacy of the flight to nature. Indeed, such talk is very much taboo. Barthian theology, appropriated widely (at least in a watered-down form) by American churches, was and remains a powerful force opposed to the flight to nature, given its radical opposition to "natural theology." The urban-oriented secular theology, with its jabs against "romanticism" in any form, also articulately discourages acceptance of the return to nature. Existentialist theology stresses man's transcendence of, and dominion over nature. The consensus in biblical studies–now significantly shaping Roman Catholic as well as Protestant thought is that authentic faith entails first and foremost a commitment to existence in history and revelation in history, not existence and revelation in nature. All this has worked to suppress public commitment in the Church, in almost any form, to the flight to nature.

Large numbers of American Christians, along with our culture as a whole, are attracted, even captivated, by the desire to flee to nature. But official theology effectively suppresses articulation of the cultural desire in an ecclesiastical context. This theological suppression, it should be noted, has not been difficult since, as we saw, the contemporary American experience of desiring to flee to nature is itself largely unarticulated. The situation is somewhat analogous to the life of the Christian Church in some parts of Latin America, where official theology has been superimposed on the native culture, prohibiting public defense of still popular native religious practices.

Beneath the surface in the life of the Church a well-spring of interest in the flight to nature has been apparent in the small town, suburban, and affluent urban sectors. The Church has tried, for one thing, to bring nature into its piety. This has happened especially at Easter, when the arrays of lilies and the sentimentalities of the typical nature-sermons have tended to obscure the true meaning of the New Testament faith in the Resurrection of Christ. In all seasons, moreover, Jesus himself has been depicted visually, in paintings and in Church publications, as the good shepherd walking through the beautiful hills of Galilee with a little lamb on his shoulders. Hardly ever has he been portrayed in popular religious art as the angry public figure who casts out the money changers from the temple. Children have been taught that "Jesus wants you for a sunbeam." And adults have grown tenaciously fond of such hymns as "Beautiful Savior," or this vivid expression of piety:

> I come to the Garden alone,
> While the dew is still on the roses.
> And the voice I hear falling on my ear
> The Son of God discloses.
> And he walks with me and he talks with me,
> And he tells me I am his own,
> And the joy we share, as we tarry there,
> None other has ever known.

Secondly, the Church has also attempted to introduce its piety into nature. It has gone *to* nature to immerse itself there, sometimes with the passion of a lost son returning home. In various ways the Church has set its worship in nature: by geographical location, with picture windows before scenic views; by establishing outdoor worship centers with such names as "the Cathedral in the Pines"; by the construction and regular use of retreat centers. But perhaps the single most important sign of the flight to nature in the life of the American Church has been the Bible camp. Churches of all varieties have established camps, usually far away from "civilization," by the side of a lake. There men and women, young and old, clergy and laity, have come together to read the Bible and to commune with God in nature. There countless numbers of young American Christians have been inspired to undertake service in the Church by a variety of sunrise, lakeside, mountaintop, sunset, and campfire experiences. Thereafter many of them have come to look back longingly at their summer camp "mountain-top experience," and continued to thirst for that kind of experience as they entered the "grubby, grimy, rat-race in the real world."

All this has been done, as I have indicated, with little or no doctrinal validation. Themes from the Scriptures and the theological tradition have been cited, to be sure, in order to justify the practice. At a "Cathedral in the Pines" worshippers would tend to find the "nature-texts" in the Bible as a matter of course. At a summer Bible camp believers would tend to talk about God the Creator as a matter of course. But apart from a few denominations, such as the Unitarian-Universalists, the practice of going to nature for spiritual food rarely has had official theological sanction. Indeed the flight to nature has been suppressed by officially accepted theology. This has led to a serious split in the religious consciousness of many American Christians. The best illustrative case is the hypothetical youngster nurtured on God-in-nature religion in Sunday School perhaps partly in the faith from *Ideals Magazine*), who then goes to summer camp and has his mountain-top experience, and who next is imbued with nature-scorning existentialist theology in seminary, on his way to service in the Church. Later on, will not his heart tell him one thing and his intellect tell him another? Which voice will he heed?

Given this practical orientation to nature in piety and to piety in nature, it is no surprise that large numbers of Christians have remained faithful to the general American cult of the simple rustic life. The life of the Church is in this respect largely indistinguishable from the life of the culture. This may help to explain why the urban-oriented secular theology has so slowly penetrated into the ecclesiastical grass roots, particularly into the suburbs. The religion most congenial to many American Christians is essentially anti-urban. The "suburban captivity" of American Churches, which Gibson Winter has analyzed, may have a number of roots,[2] but undoubtedly one of the deepest is the cult of the simple rustic life. Nature is not frequently mentioned, admittedly, in the pronouncements of a Norman Vincent Peale or a Billy Graham. But each in his own way looks back to an earlier, less complicated, and less industrialized era, the golden age of simple truths; whether they be the simple truths of positive thinking or the simple truths of conversion and the Bible. And, with little doubt, both Peale and Graham have been moving with the popular mainstream of American Church life. Peale and Graham speak for the older, unalienated generation of American Christians. Both speak for a generation of Christians whose piety is deeply rooted in the Bible-camp experience. Their proclamations say, in effect, that the rugged life, the vigorous independent way of the people on the frontier, is essentially the best way.

There can be little doubt now that this practical orientation to nature in piety and piety in nature and its concomitant immersion in the general American cult of the simple rustic life serve as a serious drag on the Church's life. How can the Church minister and serve prophetically in the contemporary world when so many of its members have a commitment that is essentially anti-urban? This is not the place to rehearse the urban-technological challenge of our time. That has already been done sufficiently well, at least in a preliminary way.[3] This is the place to note, however, that one of the chief reasons for the Church's social inertia, or at least one of the factors which continually works to cement the Church in a position of social inertia, is its practical relationship to the world of nature.

Some might urge that the best response for those who are sensitive to the contemporary urban-technological challenge is merely to intensify the critique of the flight to nature. But that would be a serious mistake. The critique should be continued, but by itself it is not enough, a point which has been amply proved by the failure of officially accepted theology to penetrate the underlying nature religion characteristic of major segments in the Church's life. What we need is *an alternative,* a theology of nature which is constructed with an awareness of the socio-economic implications of its affirmations.

2. Compulsive Manipulation and the Church's Inner Life

While the theme of Nature versus Civilization has been evident in the life of the Church chiefly as a matter of practice, conscious theological articulation has been taboo. Most of the Church's publicly professed theology has worked to counteract the interest in fleeing to nature. On the other hand, the theme of Civilization versus Nature in its contemporary form, the cult of compulsive manipulation, is in evidence not only as a matter of practice, but also to some extent as a matter of theological articulation.

The theological articulation appears in several ways. We can see it in the widespread acceptance of the "I-Thou, I-It" distinction expressed by Martin Buber; and in the equally widespread application of the I-It category to all human relationships to nature (although, ironically, Buber himself does not do this).[4] Nature, as an "It," is essentially and exclusively an object for human manipulation. Rudolf Bultmann and Karl Barth even *define* nature by its openness to manipulation (*Verfugbarkeit*).[5] For Bultmann particularly, nature is the "objective" world, the It-world, over which man should continually exercise dominion, lest he succumb to the threat of his own objectification through identification with nature.[6] The new urban-oriented theology moves in a similar direction, although it also gives some indications that there are other human relationships to nature besides the I-It relationship. Thus Cox accepts and celebrates what he feels is the characteristic modern experience of "the universe as the city of man."[7] Cox and others with similar interests take over Marxist themes, which again and again depict the world as a theatre where man should manipulate the sources of wealth for the sake of social justice. This political thrust of urban-oriented theology, which is also shared somewhat by older theologians such as Bultmann and Barth, is not in question here. What is noteworthy is the thoroughgoing emphasis on *man and his dominion* over his environment. This means that by default, if not by conscious intention, theology works to support the general American cultural theme, Civilization versus Nature.

This support is felt generally throughout the Church's life. This of course is not to suggest that the Church's theology has led directly to the pollution of nature; on the contrary, sometimes it has directly opposed it. *It is to suggest, however, that the Church's theology has not offered appreciable resources to counteract a merely exploitative approach to nature. It is also to suggest that the Church's theology has worked, sometimes quite indirectly, to encourage an exploitative approach among its own members.* One can imagine a businessman, for example, encouraged at one moment in his cult of the simple rustic life by attending a Church retreat, who at another moment is encouraged to continue a destructive strip-mining enterprise by hearing from the pulpit that nature, after all, is merely that "It-world" out there, over which man has been given dominion by God.

The Church's general theological support for the theme is intensely felt where the Church is associated with or situated in the academic world. For here, in the first place, the general cultural schizophrenia has begun to wane, if it has not disappeared altogether. People in the academic world by and large view the cult of the simple rustic life as a romanticizing escape from contemporary urban-technological life. Academic theologians generally see matters in much the same way. There is a corresponding predisposition in academic circles, moreover, in favor of a utilitarian approach to nature. The academic world, above all in its publicly supported sector, is very much in tune with the societal goal of exploiting nature to benefit mankind. This is a major purpose of the burgeoning American "multiversities." With this goal also many of the Church's theologians are in general agreement.

Further, people in the academic world are still predisposed to accept the mechanical view of nature, a phenomenon we have already noticed. And the Church's academically based theologians are tuned in to this predisposition as well, as a general rule.[8] This is frequently made explicit in discussions of miracles, where all agree that God does not interrupt the "chain of causes and effects" in nature. In the context of the academic world, then, the Church's publicly professed theology comes down hard on the side of a utilitarian view of nature supporting the contemporary cult of compulsive manipulation.

The support of theology for that cultural pattern, however, has been felt most intensely in those segments of the Church immediately and intimately involved with the challenge of urban life. In this context, the cult of the simple rustic life is seen not only as a romantic fantasy, but even more as an oppressive ideology. Where the needs of the poor and the disenfranchised are felt with a sense of urgency, it is almost inevitable that there should be profound initial sympathy for the general attitude of the poor to nature—"take what you can get." This is essentially the utilitarian approach in a revolutionary context. A rural priest in Appalachia may care little about the destruction of a beautiful valley not far from his parish if the new dam will bring cheap electricity and new jobs into his district.

This varied ecclesiastical involvement with the cult of compulsive manipulation leads to some deleterious results in the life of the Church. The most obvious is the unthinking tolerance of those very patterns of national life which support the defacement and pollution of nature. That is serious enough, but it is not all. Subtly but relentlessly, *the cult of compulsive manipu-*

lation is sapping the vitality from the internal life of the Church itself. This becomes apparent when we examine the three central theological "virtues" of the Church, its *faith,* its *hope,* and its *love,* and when we look at the Church's *biblical interpretation.*

The utilitarian approach to nature weakens the *faith* of the Church, especially its faith considered as its *justification.* Regin Prenter observes that we continue to speak as Luther did about justification by faith alone and the uselessness of our own works for salvation. "All this is preached from the pulpit," Prenter notes, "sung in our hymns, and taught in catechetical instruction. . . . But,–and this is the strange part about it–the great liberation of the earthly life, so inextricably bound up with this gospel for the Reformers, is missing." [9] Luther and Calvin took their hearers' sympathetic relation to the world of nature for granted when they preached justification by grace through faith. In their time men of faith could sense the presence and activity of God in nature, as well as in history. It was not difficult to receive a rainstorm, for example, as a good gift coming immediately from the hand of God. Nor was it difficult to sense the wrath of God, the immediate, actual Divine displeasure, in an earthquake or in a famine. "If anything adverse happens," Calvin says of the man of faith, "straightway he will raise up his mind here also unto God, whose hand can best impress patience and peaceful moderation of mind upon us." Here he means to include such natural calamities as fire and famine. "When that light of divine providence has once shone upon a godly man," Calvin explains, "he is then relieved and set free not only from the extreme anxiety and fear that were pressing him before, but from every care." [10] That is to say, having heard in the preaching of justification by grace through faith alone that my salvation is sure and certain, that "it is finished," that I need do nothing or suffer nothing to obtain it, I can learn to sense that the same God of grace and power is at work in, and controls finally, my environment. This kind of *outer sense* frees me from all care.

But if I cannot sense God's activity in the world around me, then its calamities, big and small, the earthquake or the fall of a nest of birds from a tree, become a threat to the peace of my salvation. Instead of seeing the inscrutable hand of *my* God directly at work in such disturbing events, I tend to see fate, chance, or impersonal power. Hence there will be little or no sense of "liberation of my earthly life." Today under the influence of the utilitarian view of nature, this sense of liberation must be an almost exclusively *inner sense* of the one who hears the Word of justification. The outer sense, the sense for nature, is cut away, and faith is internalized and spiritualized. It is no wonder that many find it difficult to reproduce in themselves the vibrant faith which so guided the lives of the Reformers.

The faith of the Church also involves *sanctification,* the transformation of daily life. This touches on the province of vocation and daily prayer, so important to the Reformers. For them justification was never without sanctification. They underscored the Pauline idea that every Christian is a new creation (II Cor. 2:17). Erasmus' image of the plowman, happy at work with Psalms on his lips, is close to the Reformation understanding of sanctification. Luther, for example, writes with deep conviction about the intimate, gracious, and powerful presence of God in the sphere of daily experience:

> What however is all our work in the field, in the garden, in the city, in the house, in defense, in ruling before God? What is it other than a kind of child's play through which God wants to give his gifts to field, house and everywhere? All these are the masks of our Lord God; he wants to remain hidden under these masks and to work everything.[11]

For those who have accepted the utilitarian view of nature, however, the image of man working or playing with a deep sense for the gracious, powerful presence of God is almost idyllic fancy. Their leisure time may be set in the "wide outdoors," and they may use the world of fields and trees and mountains as a "breathing spell." But somehow it remains isolated from that sphere of existence in which they seek to establish meaning for their lives, from any sphere in which they look for the gracious, powerful presence of God.

What is true for leisure time is also true for daily work. In recent years many have traced the meaninglessness of daily work to its increasing mechanization.[12] Delimited and controlled by machines, work becomes drudgery. The machine is "out there," isolated from that sphere of existence in which we seek to establish meaning for our lives, isolated from that sphere in which we look for God and his gifts. The machine in this respect is, as it were, a mere extension of the foreign world of nature. In the minds of those who accept the utilitarian view, both nature, already delimited as a machine, and the actual man-made world of machines coalesce into one alien world. The only remaining realm of meaning is neither the physical milieu of leisure not the physical context of work, but the sphere of inter-personal relations. This is one of the major reasons why depth psychology and existential philosophy have had such an impact on the Church. Many who are deeply concerned with persons and with history in general tend to scorn mere "things."

It is not easy for people to *pray* when they are isolated from their material environment. The modern urban or academic churchman, understandably and symbolically, must shut his eyes while he prays. His piety must depend almost entirely on his inner sense for God's presence and glory. For, if he looks about him he can neither see God's glory nor sense God's presence. So, increasingly, prayer becomes an isolated sacred act, an act which has no place in the "secular" world.[13] Prayer is separated from work and leisure. Work and leisure are separated from prayer. Not *all* of this, to be sure, is due to acceptance of the utilitarian view of nature, but part of it surely is.

So acceptance of the utilitarian view undermines *faith* by weakening our sense of justification and bifurcating our sense of sanctification. But more than our faith is affected; *Hope* is also damaged (a point which apparently has not been explored by the new theologians of hope). The early Fathers and later thinkers like Calvin frequently drew attention to the power God exercises in nature in order to make it possible for the faithful to hope for their own resurrection and for the renewal of the whole world. As Calvin says, "It is difficult to believe that bodies when consumed with rottenness, will at length be raised up in their season." [14] Yet nature, where the omnipotence of God is displayed, teaches this very thing. In this sense, *natura spirat resurrectionem.*[15] The resurrection of the body would not be so hard to believe, Calvin explains, "If we paid proper attention to the miracles thrust before our eyes throughout the world." Indeed, the Reformer continues, "no one is truly persuaded of the coming resurrection unless he is seized with wonder, and ascribes to the power of God its due glory." [16]

This motif appears more explicitly in the earlier Fathers. Here the remarks of the First Epistle of Clement are typical:

Let us consider, beloved, how the Lord continually proves to us that there shall be a future resurrection, of which he has rendered the Lord Jesus Christ the first-fruits by raising Him from the dead. Let us contemplate, beloved, the resurrection which is at all times taking place. Day and night declare to us a resurrection. The night sinks to sleep, and the day arises; the day departs, and the night comes on. Let us behold the fruits [of the earth], how the sowing of grain takes place. The sower goes forth, and casts it into the ground; and the seed being thus scattered, though dry and naked when it fell upon the earth, is gradually dissolved. Then out of its dissolution the mighty power of the providence of the Lord raises it up again, and from one seed many arise and bring forth fruit.[17]

St. Paul, of course, employed the analogy of sown seed to interpret death and resurrection (cf. I Cor. 15:35-38). This is the same Paul who held that God's "eternal power and deity" are "clearly perceived in the things that have been made" (Rom. 1:20). Jesus used a similar image in explaining the coming and the miraculous growth of the Kingdom of God (Mt. 13:31f). And as C. H. Dodd has said concerning Jesus' parables, "the Kingdom of God is *intrinsically like* the processes of nature and the daily life of men. Jesus therefore did not feel the need of making up artificial illustrations for the truths he wanted to teach. He found them ready made by the Maker of man and nature." [18]

Those who have accepted the utilitarian view have little sense of God's immediate working in the world of nature. It is not easy for them to apprehend God's hand in the motion of the planets or the growth of a seed. *Hence they lack meaningful analogies for the resurrection.* It is no surprise that the early Church's very concrete resurrection faith—the Apostolic Creed has *resurrectio carnis,* even more definite than the New Testament's "resurrection of the body"—is difficult for us to understand and appropriate.[19] Many people in the church today do not easily sense the power of God over the whole of nature, including their bodies. A taproot of the hope which enlivened the early Church has withered away. This is especially discomforting in a time when our whole natural existence (and our historical existence) stands under the threat of thermo-nuclear or ecological annihilation. Compared to this threat, a weak hope is no hope at all.

Such a weakened hope means that a debilitated *love* is not far away. As Joseph Sittler has noted, if redemption does not include the whole of man's experience and environment, then there is and will always remain something of evil to be overcome. And more: "The actual man in his existence will be tempted to reduce the redemption of man to what purgation, transformation, forgiveness and blessedness is available by an 'angelic' escape from the cosmos of natural and historical fact." [20] Men cannot easily live lovingly in a world which has not been claimed wholly by God's love. Why, it may be asked, care for the bodily existence of the starving brother, if that existence is doomed to ultimate annihilation? St. Paul knew of this kind of question. "If the dead are not raised," he answered bluntly, " 'Let us eat and drink, for tomorrow we die' " (I Cor. 15:32). Acceptance of the utilitarian view of nature thus leads to a weak hope, and a weak hope, in turn, leads to an emaciated ethic.

From another perspective, man's love for his brother entails an acceptance of, and a commitment to, the integrity of the brother's corporality. In this respect as in others, the Good Samaritan is a paradigm of authentic Christian love. He gives paramount attention to the bodily ills of the man fallen among thieves. But what if a man who wishes to love his brother cannot relate himself with respect to a tree or a mountain or to a computer? It seems likely that his ability to relate himself positively to all physical beings, including men, will be diminished. Here the warning of George H. Williams is pertinent. He writes,

> Unless some believers in every generation can, through the poverty by which we divest ourselves of all lordliness, join St. Francis in his canticle addressed to the sun and the bears as brethren, . . . then in the present stage of mankind's awesome capacity for enforcing lordship over nature—whether in ruthless urbanization of the

countryside, or in exploitation of natural resources heedless of generations to come, or in any careless experimentation in the realm of life, disease, and death—we shall presently find that we can no longer address even one another as brother and sister and that a utilitarian view of nature will have blasted our human nature.[21]

Our relation to nature and our love for our fellows are intimately related. When the first suffers, the other will suffer, too.

The ongoing life of the Church, its faith, its hope, and its love, is thus threatened by acceptance of the utilitarian view of nature. One might even liken this acceptance to a cancerous infection. It does not suddenly and dramatically affect the body, but little by little it saps strength and vitality. Through a number of symptoms, it declares that something essential is not functioning properly.

Closely related to the whole problem of the Church's relation to nature is the question of contemporary *biblical interpretation* within the Church. Acceptance of the utilitarian view seems to be undercutting the vitality and breadth of the Church's ongoing exposition of Scripture. Every honest parish minister knows that he must interpret biblical texts which sometimes accent such miraculous events as Jesus' walking on the water. Above all, the resurrection must be interpreted. And the resurrection, as the New Testament views it, is firmly rooted in the world of nature.[22] It is no wonder that the demythologizing program of Rudolf Bultmann continues to receive such widespread attention in the contemporary Church, for Bultmann directs his attention precisely to the problem foremost in the minds of most preachers today. Bultmann responds to the modern preacher's pathos: the desire to preach with power to men who do not share the world view of the New Testament. At the same time, Bultmann illustrates how abortive modern biblical interpretation can become. These points need elaboration.

Almost lost in the heat of the debate over demythologization is the fact that its chief exponent employs a certain idea of *nature* as a criterion for what is mythological and what is not mythological. In a discussion of miracle, for example, Bultmann remarks:

> The idea of the mysterious event (*Wunder*) as miracle (*Mirakel*) has become untenable for us today because we understand natural occurrences as lawful happenings and therefore we understand a miracle as a suspension of the lawful totality of natural occurrences. We cannot hold to the latter idea today.

The thought of nature's lawfulness, Bultmann concludes, "is given with our existence in the world." [23] He has recently restated this point, with direct reference to his program of demythologizing and with regard to certain developments in contemporary natural science (the discovery of a kind of unlawfulness in the subatomic world). After outlining what he considers to be the mythological conception of the world in the New Testament, he comments:

> This conception of the world we call mythological because it is different from the conception of the world which has been formed and developed by science since its inception in ancient Greece and which has been accepted by all modern man. *In this modern conception of the world the cause-and-effect nexus is fundamental.* Although modern physical theories take account of chance in the chain of cause and effect in subatomic phenomena, our daily living, purposes and actions are not affected. In any case, modern science does not believe that the course of nature can be interrupted or, so to speak, perforated, by supernatural powers.[24]

Bultmann evidently structures his demythologizing on the presupposition of a mechanistic view of nature. Whatever seems to be inexplicable in terms of this view of nature is mythological and should therefore be set aside or interpreted in terms of man's (historical) self-understanding.[25]

The result of Bultmann's program is, in part, as follows: Jesus' exorcism of demons from the sick can have no meaning for us because sickness can be understood in terms of natural causation. The New Testament's mythical eschatology–the picture of an apocalyptic disruption and renewal of all things–is untenable because even if we believe that the world as we know it will come to an end in time, we expect the end to be a natural catastrophe, not mythical as for the New Testament. The corporeal resurrection of Jesus cannot make sense to us (!), because we cannot conceive how God can bring life by the resuscitation of a corpse. Finally, we cannot understand the death of Christ both as a sacrifice *and* a cosmic event (Christ portrayed as defeating cosmic powers), because for us human life is distinctive precisely because it is *not* determined by cosmic powers, because it is fundamentally a matter of free decision.[26]

There is reason to ask if Bultmann's is the only honest alternative available, for it appears that his way entails the discarding of much of what the early Church considered to be essential, with serious ramifications for the Church today. We have already noticed some of these ramifications, especially in discussing the Church's hope. In this connection, one can wonder whether a resurrected Christ who is not in some sense corporally resurrected, is anything more than a phantom. If so, is it not most honest to stop speaking about the "resurrection faith" altogether? In terms applicable to the whole of contemporary theology, Richard R. Niebuhr has expressed some reservations many feel when they read Bultmann:

What cannot be thought as occurring in nature cannot be conceived as an historical event, in the ordinary sense. Consequently, it is necessary to find a wholly transcendental kind of history, unrelated to the space-time continuum, in which a home can be provided for the miracles that have been exiled from mundane history.

When Christianity is coupled with such a dualism, it loses practically all of its original substance, and, instead of looking to Jesus Christ as God's promise of the restoration of the whole natural-historical order, it concentrates on a spiritualized Christ who is utterly irrelevent to our natural, social existence.[27]

What would become of Bultmann's program if viable, alternative ideas of nature were available? Surely it would not collapse, but just as surely it would have to be modified. Employing another interpretation of nature, for example, we might be able to accept some of Jesus' healings as meaningful for us. It might be possible, too, to allow that the resurrection of Jesus Christ has a certain objective foundation in nature, as well as powerful subjective import for the believer. In other words, Bultmann's very serious program,–serious because the life of the Church is sustained by its exposition of the Bible,–might be able to proceed more persuasively if it could draw on an interpretation of nature other than a mechanistic view.

Presently, however, Bultmann and those who follow him seem to hold a mechanistic view of nature. This is the fateful concomitant of acceptance of the utilitarian view of nature: the Church has apparently been forced to depend heavily for its biblical interpretation on that very conception of nature which is a source of considerable malaise in its ongoing life. So, in addition to everything else, acceptance of the utilitarian view undercuts the vitality and breadth of the Church's exposition of Scripture. The reverse, of course, is also true. An apparently truncated biblical exegesis only serves to cement the acceptance of the cult of compulsive manipulation.

To summarize: Nature is problematic within the Church, then, in two major respects, first with regard to the Church's attitude toward society, secondly with regard to the Church's own inner life.

In the first respect nature is a problem insofar as the Church has participated in, and thereby reenforced, the general cultural schizophrenia with regard to nature. On the one hand, that has meant acceptance of the flight to nature and the cult of the simple rustic life, with a concomitant social escapism. The cult of the simple rustic life *has* been opposed by the Church's publicly professed theology, but in the main with an only superficial success.

On the other hand, the Church's participation in the general cultural schizophrenia has meant acceptance of the cult of compulsive manipulation with the concomitant tendency of ecological indifference. This development has been supported by the Church's publicly professed theology, insofar as that theology has presupposed, and sometimes proposed, a utilitarian approach to nature. Significantly, the Church's official theology has found an especially sympathetic audience in the growing and increasingly influential academic and non-affluent urban sectors of the Church—sectors which are now passing beyond or have already passed beyond the general cultural schizophrenia to a stage where, by default or intention, the emphasis is placed entirely on the utilitarian approach to nature.

Nature is a problem for the Church, secondly, in its internal life to the degree that the cult of compulsive manipulation has been accepted. Again, such acceptance has been noticeable particularly in the academic and non-affluent urban sectors of the Church. The acceptance of an exploitative approach to nature with the support of its theology is seriously sapping the vitality of the Church's own inner life, its faith, its hope, and its love, and apparently its ongoing biblical interpretation as well.

The contemporary situation requires a new theological approach to nature not only because nature poses a serious dilemma for society in general, as we saw in chapters one and two, but also because that dilemma is very much in evidence within the life of the Church itself, with serious consequences for the household of faith: retardation of the Church's political involvement in society and undermining of the Church's own inner life. Our massive social-ecological crisis is complemented by an extensive ecclesiastical-ecological crisis. And the deepest roots of both seem to be intertwined.

Surprisingly, we must conclude, the Church like society in general has been unwilling consistently to face the challenge of historical existence. All too often it has gone after the gods of nature, turning its back on the poor in the slums. In like manner, all too frequently it has accepted the ways of Mammon, allowing both the earth and its inhabitants to be manipulated and exploited. The Church needs no less urgently than society as a whole to hear anew the message of the Bible, where the dilemma of Nature versus Civilization and Civilization versus Nature is resolved. If it does not hear, it will surely and shortly find that its history, along with the history of society at large, has been irreparably damaged.

IV. Beyond the Dilemma: The Biblical Vision

Anyone who has heard biblical scholars discuss with natural scientists the relation of religion and science knows well that one cannot simply page through the Bible and come up with answers to modern scientific questions. The world-views of the biblical writer and of the modern scientist are poles apart. What is true for science is all the more true for modern culture. The substance and the shape of modern culture—our existential concerns and ways of thinking—contrast sharply with the substance and shape of biblical culture. And biblical culture, somehow leaving *our* myths, presuppositions, and the Scriptures covers millenia. The "biblical world-view" is by no means a self-evident unity.

This means that we cannot simply turn to the Bible to read how to resolve our modern societal and ecclesiastical dilemmas with nature. Even the concept "nature" cannot easily be identified in biblical writings—so far is our culture removed from the biblical mind. We can never really jump out of our own culture, somehow leaving *our* myths, presuppositions, and values behind. But, mindful of the exacting methods and the cumulative results of historical scholarship wherever possible, we can venture to soar imaginatively to the strange but alluring world of biblical faith in order to discover new or forgotten themes and ideas.

It would obviously be preferable at this point if we could simply summarize the work of biblical scholarship (particularly in the contemporary period) which deals with the biblical approach to nature. But, for reasons which we need not consider here, "nature" as a theme with its own import has not directly concerned most biblical scholars to this very day.[1] The most we can hope for in this brief space, accordingly, is to be able to identify some of the major configurations in the biblical picture of nature. But the allure of that biblical picture is sufficient to make even such tentative results worth the effort.

We should be aware, however, that the biblical picture of nature has not only been neglected in scholarly study, but frequently *obscured,* especially by certain prominent theologians. The problem has been an overly narrow focus. Karl Barth is typical in this respect when he states that *the* interest of the biblical writers is God's activity in relation to *man.* In similar vein Emil Brunner remarks that "the cosmic element in the Bible is never anything more than the 'scenery' in which the history of mankind takes place."[2] A more generous consideration will show, however, that the writers of the Old and New Testaments by no means think of nature as mere scenery for the Divinely directed drama of man's creation and salvation. Although man is surely the central actor, as Barth and Brunner have rightly emphasized, nature itself has its own distinct role to play in the Divine drama. The God witnessed to in the Bible plays out a *history with nature,* as well as a history with man. Together these two histories, inseparable yet distinct, comprise the Universal Divine Story of creation, redemption, and consummation.

The *main lines* of the biblical picture of the Divine history with nature are set forth in both Testaments, but most of the *details* of the picture come from the Old Testament. But in its main lines, the New Testament is consistent with the Old, and that continuity is decisive. Of subordinate significance is the fact that many of the details concerning nature found in the Old Testament are taken for granted by the New, particularly in the teaching of Jesus. That we find most of the colors and the lesser lines of the biblical picture of nature in the Old Testament, then, should present no difficulty if we take our stand with the classical tradition of the Church and approach the *whole* Bible as Scripture.

1. The Beginning

The prelude to the Divine history with nature is the *act of creation.* As Jürgen Moltmann and Wolfhart Pannenberg have recently emphasized, however, in the Bible creation is not an isolated event or end in itself: it is a beginning which looks forward to the final goal of all things, the consummated Kingdom of God. The alpha has meaning, in other words, only insofar as it is directed toward the omega. Creation is not just "back there"; creation is this present world as it is determined by, and moving toward, the Final Future of God.[3] This motif is especially pronounced in the New Testament where an apocalyptic framework predominates. It is to be seen too in the non-apocalyptic "creation hymn" of Colossians 1:15ff. Here creation and redemption are inextricably intertwined: the created order exists and subsists in and for Christ the redeemer. On the other hand, subordinated as it may be to redemption, creation is not passed over lightly or demeaned by the biblical writers. This is especially clear in the Old Testament, although the New Testament, too, (in contrast to Gnosticism) has this sense for the integrity and goodness of the created order.

There is no doubt that in the creation narratives of Genesis the focus is on man. He is clearly in the center of the stage, especially in the second narrative (Gen. 2:4ff.). So too in the first, the so-called priestly account (Gen. 1:1-2:3), man is the apex; creation is incomplete without him. Yet in this first narrative we can also discern the beginnings of another theme, God's history with nature.

For the priestly writer and for the Bible generally, God creates nature in order to bless man, to make a congenial place for his history with man. Yet God also is depicted as creating nature *for the sake of his own enjoyment*. As S. R. Driver has observed, a note of Divine satisfaction runs through the whole Priestly narrative of creation. This is part of the significance of the expression, "And God saw that it was good." "The formula used marks each work as one corresponding to the Divine intention, perfect, as for its nature required and permitted, complete, and the object of the Creator's approving regard and satisfaction." [4]

In Genesis 1:31, immediately following the completion of God's creative activity with the creation of man, the words "*very* good" are used for the first time. It might be assumed that these words imply that God bestows superior approval on the creature for whose sake he began to create the world. But such an interpretation would be too narrow. The "very good" of Genesis 1:31 refers to the whole: "and God saw *everything* that he had made and behold it was very good." The text does not suggest that God sees man *alone* as very good. Of course the creation would not be "very good," according to the Priestly writer, without man. But—and this is the point—neither would it be "very good" without the whole of nature. When God looks at all the results of his creative activity he takes joy in every thing he sees.

The Psalmist states this idea in more vivid terms. After enumerating God's creative works throughout the whole world, in words like these:

Thou makest springs gush forth in the valleys:
they flow between the hills,
they give drink to every beast of the field:
the wild asses quench their thirst.
(Ps. 104:10f.)

May the glory of the Lord endure forever,
may the Lord rejoice in his works.
(v. 31)[5]

The same poet also refers to the raison d'être of the monster of the deep, the Leviathan:

There go the ships,
and the Leviathan which thou didst form to sport with it.
(v. 26)[6]

God creates the sea monsters to play with them! We might venture to render this thought in modern idiom by saying that God created the extra-galactic nebulae to play with them.

The teaching of Jesus presupposes this theme that God rejoices in his creative works: "Consider the lilies of the field, how they grow; they neither toil nor spin, yet I tell you that Solomon in all his glory was not arrayed like one of these" (Mt. 6:29). Commenting on this text and others like it, T. W. Manson remarked, "God clothes the lilies of the field and feeds the birds, one might almost say, because God is fond of beautiful flowers and fond of birds." [7] Manson also ties this motif suggestively to the central New Testament concern with self-giving love (e.g. Phil. 2): The statement "He that would be chief among you must be servant of all," Manson observes, has its applications for the Creator of all no less than for men. The heavenly Father remembers and serves all his creatures.

The conviction that God creates nature so that he might take joy in it and serve all his creatures helps to explain why a poem like Psalm 29 can virtually ignore man in its celebration of Yahweh's works. Borrowed from Canaanite religion it might have been, but this Psalm *was borrowed,* and fittingly. Here as elsewhere the biblical writers presuppose that God has a relation to nature distinct from his intimate relation to man, that nature has worth to God apart from its role in the Divine-human drama. God is even viewed in the Old Testament as *making a covenant with nature.* Thus Noah is directed: "Of every living thing of all flesh, you shall bring two of them of every sort into the ark" (Gen. 6:19). And after the flood Noah is told:

> Behold, I establish my covenant with you and your descendents after you, *and with every living creature that is with you.*[8]

If it is suggested that God makes his covenant with the animals solely in order to bless man by providing him food, one may ask why God would direct Noah to take *every* kind of animal into the ark, even the unclean (cf. Gen. 7:2, 8).

Given God's special interest in nature, each created being is depicted as having a certain integrity, a life of its own with God. Every natural entity, first of all, has its own *place.*[9] Nature is established not on a tentative basis, as it were, as though it might exhaust its goodness in service of man. Creation is structured by the wisdom of the architect, with each part having its own role and sphere (cf. Prov. 16:4). So the high mountains are for the wild goats and the rocks are for the badgers (Ps. 104:18). And from their individual places all things look to their Creator: "The young lions roar for their prey seeking their food from God" (Ps. 104:21; cf. 145:15f.; Job 38:39-41). From their appointed places all things are seen or heard to sing, quite apart from the being or well-being of man: The outgoings of the morning and evening shout for joy (Ps. 65:8b). The sun comes forth like a bridegroom leaving his chamber and like a strong man runs its course with joy (Ps. 19:5). Long before the creation of man, when the foundations of the earth were being laid, the morning stars sang together (Job 38:7a). A closely related theme is that the whole world, nature as well as man, worships God (Ps. 89:5; 96:9; Is. 43:20a; 66:23).[10] It is a clear implication that nature's singing and worship of God are enjoyable or pleasing to him—just as the right kind of sacrifice is sometimes said to be pleasing to God.[11]

Nature's intrinsic worth in the eyes of God is further reflected in the idea that man, notwithstanding his dominion over it, should respect nature. Man's dominion is not unlimited: "a righteous man has regard for the life of his beast" (Ps. 12:10). Israel is commanded not to crossbreed cattle (Lev. 19:19; Dt. 22:9-11) and not to destroy the young in a wild bird's nest (Dt. 22:6f.). Similarly, the land should lie fallow on the seventh year so the poor *and* the wild beasts can eat (Ex. 23:10f.); an ox is not to be muzzled when it treads grain (Dt. 25:4). Man also has the positive responsibility to till the earth and keep it (cf. Gen. 2:5).

This relation of respect is not understood as an alien duty stemming from a hard command, that is, as a joyless obligation. Rather, the respect is understood to involve *wonder,* even delight. This is the mood of the Psalmist:

> O Lord, how manifold are thy works!
> In wisdom has thou made them all;
> the earth is full of thy creatures.
> Yonder is the sea, great and wide,
> which teems with things innumerable,
> living things both small and great.
> (Ps. 104:24f.)

Similarly, the heavens "tell the glory of God":

> In them he has set a tent for the sun,
> which comes forth like a bridegroom leaving his chamber,
> and like a strong man runs its course in joy.
> Its rising is from the end of the heavens,
> and its circuit to the end of them;
> and there is nothing hid from its head.
>
> (Ps. 19:5f.)

The thirty-eighth through the fortieth chapters of the book of Job contain passages akin to these, although there the mood of wonder is qualified not so much by delight as by a fearful awe.

It is of course true that man's wonder is inseparably related in these texts to the awareness of God's wonderful activity in nature. But the wondering *is* directed to *nature*. Moreover, the distinction between the activity of God and natural processes, while never forgotten, is by no means pronounced. Light, for example, is said to be the garment of the majestic God, and the clouds his chariot (Ps. 104:2,3).

Another pertinent Old Testament notion is the idea of the reflected Divine glory. God is pictured as crowning *man* with glory and honor (Ps. 8:5b; Ex. 34:29); behind this conviction, perhaps, is the idea that man's creation according to the image of God constitutes a reflection of the Divine glory. But this reflection is not something in which man alone is involved. And this is the decisive point here. Indeed, God fills the whole earth (Is. 6:1-3) and also the heavens (Ps. 19:1) with his glory. The Divine majesty is evident in the midst of the elemental forces (cf. Ps. 29:3). Paul stands in this Old Testament tradition when he refers to the "eternal power and deity" of God as being manifest in "the things that have been made"

(Rom. 1:20). This theme of God's glory manifest throughout the whole creation is congruent with all the other themes suggesting that nature in itself has its own value and integrity in his eyes, quite apart from its other function as a vehicle of blessing for man. The God to whom the biblical writers bear witness is One who rejoices in all his works.

2. The Focus of the History—The Final Fulfillment

Creation is not just an isolated beginning, according to biblical thought, but is this world proceeding toward the consummated Kingdom of God. This future reference was present in Israel's early covenant faith in the conviction that Yahweh will in time fulfill his promises faithfully.[12] But the interest in the future developed considerably during and after the time of the monarchy. Against the tendency to identify the political and physical kingdom of Israel with the Kingdom of Yahweh, with an accompanying hope for a "Day of the Lord" when all Israel's enemies and ills would finally disappear, the prophets proclaimed that the Day of the Lord would be a time of radical judgment–for Israel too. "This meant," John Bright has stated, "that the hope of the establishment of the Kingdom of God–the hope embodied in the dream of the Day of Yahweh –began to be divorced from the Israelite state and driven beyond it."[13] It is characteristic of the Old Testament that nature should be included in this new conception:

> Behold the day of the Lord comes,
> cruel, with wrath and fierce anger,
> to make the earth a desolation
> and to destroy sinners from it.
> For the stars of the heavens and their constellations
> will not give light,

the sun will be dark at its rising
and the moon will not shed its light.
I will punish the world for its evil.
(Is. 13:9-11)[14]

The prophets generally were convinced, however, that the Day of Yahweh would not be the last act of God, that they could look forward also to a restoration of Israel's fortunes (cf. Zeph. 3:20; Obadaiah 21; Zech. 14:16). Isaiah envisioned a new David who would rule over a new Israel (Is. 9:1-7). Elsewhere a messianic figure is also seen as the signal of Israel's restoration (Mic. 6:1ff.; Jer. 23:5ff.; Ez. 17:22; Is. 45:1ff.).[15] It is again characteristic that the Day of restoration will be a new Day for nature, too (Joel 2:18-23).[16] Isaiah relates this to the new David (Is. 11:1-9). The theme of the coming renewal of nature is proclaimed with fervor by Deutero-Isaiah and his school:

For you shall go out in joy,
and be led forth in peace;
the mountains and hills before you
shall break forth into singing. . . .
Instead of the thorn shall come up the cypress;
instead of the briar shall come up the myrtle.
(Is. 55:12f.)

Behold, I am doing a new thing. . . .
I will make a way in the wilderness,
rivers in the desert.
The wild beast will honor me . . .
for I give water in the wilderness, . . .
to give drink to my chosen people.
(Is. 43:19f.)[17]

Then the climactic proclamation:

For behold, I create new heavens
and a new earth.

(Is. 65:17a)

But this great hope was not fulfilled in the time of the monarchy. The new creation did not occur. So the hope for the renewal of all things was pushed beyond the time of this world to a transcendent End. This occurred in the apocalyptic writings,[18] a legitimate outgrowth of Israel's faith, which, "in times of darkest despair, when the kingdoms of this earth exercised their tyrannical and unbroken rule, kept alive Israel's confidence in the triumphant Kingdom of God." [19] As Yahweh's creative and redemptive rule came to be futurized, so interest in God's history with nature tended to be focused there, too. The prophetic proclamation of a new creation was universalized to include the whole cosmos.

The coming of the Final Day is a central theme in the teaching of Jesus. Study of the "parables of growth" shows that he conceived of the Kingdom of God as coming in two stages, first, in his own words and works, second, in a final world-consummation.[20] This final day, as Jesus depicted it, would be not just the end of the world ("heaven and earth shall pass away"), but the coming of a new world (*palingenesia*).[21] More generally in the New Testament, the mission of Jesus is thought of in terms of a new creation, not solely to save mankind (after the fashion of a Gnostic redeemer). According to C. F. Burney and Matthew Black, the writings of Luke, Paul, and John all presuppose that "the appearance of Jesus Christ on earth is a new creation, to be compared with the first creation of the world and mankind." [22] Regarding the Second Gospel, moreover, "we cannot doubt that in Mk. 4:35 [-41] and 5:1-20 the incarnation is thought of as a new creation." [23]

The idea of the new creation is strikingly evident in the writings of Paul. It is implied by his use of the "Second Adam" terminology (cf. Rom. 5) and by his direct references: "Therefore, if any one is in Christ, he is a new creation; the old has passed away, behold, the new has come" (II Cor. 5:17; cf. Gal. 6:15). Paul believed that "the form of this world is passing away" (I Cor. 7:31b) and that the "creation itself will be set free from its bondage to decay and obtain the glorious liberty of the children of God" (Rom. 8:21). He took it for granted, accordingly, that the descendants of Abraham "should inherit *the world*" (Rom. 4:13; cf. Rom. 8:32; I Cor. 1:21-23). Elsewhere in the New Testament the passing of the whole world (Mr. 5:18; Mk. 13:24-27; Acts 2:19; II Pet. 3:7; Heb. 1:11; Rev. 21:1) and the coming of a new heaven and new earth (Heb. 1:12; II Pet. 3:13; Rev. 21:1, 5) are also affirmed.

Nor should we lose sight of the implications of early Christian worship. In the New Testament milieu, as N. A. Dahl has remarked, it is "highly symbolical that the Jews celebrate the Sabbath, pointing to the fulfilment of creation, whereas the Christians celebrate the first day of the week, pointing to the beginning of the new creation by the Resurrection of our Lord." [24] Oscar Cullmann has made the similar observation that in celebrating the presence of the risen Lord the early Church was confronting in Christ "the miracle of the new creation expected at the end." "This is a new creation of matter, an incorruptible matter. Nowhere else in the world is there this new spiritual body—only here in Christ." [25] This proleptic presence of the new creation in the risen Lord is in turn seen to affect the very bodies of the faithful. "It can be asserted with confidence," Cullmann continues, "that to Paul the spiritual body of Christ present in the company gathered for the meal exerts influences on the human body." Thus the eucharistic meal functions as the supreme anticipation of the end, at which time the life-giver, the Spirit—who now dwells in and enlivens the Church—will create all things new.[26]

The prophetic and apocalyptic proclamation of the new

heaven and the new earth corresponds to the general biblical motif that God creates nature not just for man, but also for God's own purposes, for his own enjoyment. For nature too will be renewed in the future, since *it has its own value in God's eyes*. Hence it is quite wrong to say, "The material universe is only the temporary removable setting of the Divine-human drama. It does not possess permanent worth." [27] If that were true for biblical thought, nature would indeed be discarded at the very end (as in Gnostic systems). But the biblical writers do not see nature slipping away into nothingness at the Final Day. Rather they affirm that it is to be renewed and transformed, as man will be renewed and transformed. God has a plan for nature as well as for man; he has a history with nature as well as with man. He creates it so that he might bring it to fulfillment, not only in order to provide the scenery for human history. Man and the whole of nature look forward to consummation in the Kingdom of God; both are established at the very beginning with reference to that Future.

This theme appears most sharply in the New Testament in the formulaic use of the expression "all things," *ta panta* (Rom. 11:36, Col. 1:15ff., Rev. 1:4 et al). Man may occupy the center of the stage in the universal Divine drama (particularly in the Gospel of John), but the New Testament holds firmly to the notion that all things flow together from God and his self-giving love in Christ toward the last act of the Divine drama, the new creation of all things.

3. The Present Shape of the History

Along with this emphasis on nature as having its own worth for God as a created work to be fulfilled in the consummated Kingdom, we meet a strong emphasis in both Testaments on the *present* creative and redemptive rule of God throughout his whole creation. God works powerfully and graciously everywhere to bring his creation to its intended fulfillment. This essential element in the biblical view needs to be highlighted, lest we misinterpret the biblical God as a watchmaker who sets things in motion and then just retires into the distant past or waits in the distant future.

In the Old Testament we meet a picture of a majestic, ever-triumphing God who holds the earth in the palm of his hand (Ps. 96:3). He is the everlasting King (Jer. 10:10), the everlasting Creator (Is. 40:28). The supreme power of his Lordship is unquestioned. According to the Chronicler:

> Thine O Lord, is the greatness, and the power and the glory, and the victory, and the majesty; for all that is in the heavens and in the earth is thine; thine is the Kingdom, O Lord, and thou art exalted as head above all (I Chr. 29:11).

Apart from God's active rule, the whole creation is unstable and impermanent. It is "as nothing" (Dan. 4:34b-35). It is a fragile space surrounded by primeval waters and thereby intrinsically open to chaos.[28] The heavens could easily vanish like smoke and the earth wear out like a garment (cf. Is. 51:6; Ps. 102:25-28). Creation is what it is only because Yahweh has stretched out the heavens and laid the foundations of the earth in the midst of the primeval waters (Ps. 24:1f.; Is. 40:22; 51:16). Given the fragile character of the whole creation and the threat of chaos, the only hope for an ordered life ("order" in the sense of peace, *shalom*) lies in Yahweh's continuing exercise of his sovereignty over chaos (Ps. 10:12, 15f.; 29;10f.; 96:10).

God, in the perspective of the Old Testament, is thus the present source and ground of all the processes of nature. Nature is not a self-enclosed, self-sufficient reality, but totally dependent from moment to moment on God's power and presence. Thus the powerful voice of the Lord breaks the cedars of Lebanon and shakes the wilderness (Ps. 29:4f., 8); it shakes the heavens and the earth (Ps. 68:7; 114:7; Jer. 10:10; Joel 3:16). Yahweh calls forth the waters of the seas and waters the land (Am. 5:8; 9:5); he rebukes the sea and makes it dry (Nahum 1:4); he withholds the spring rains (Jer. 3:3); he commands the stars in the heavens (Is. 45:12); he gives the blessings of breast and womb (Gen. 29:31); he sends thunder and rain in answer to prayer (I Sam. 12:18); he feeds the wild beasts and all animals (Ps. 104:27f.; 145:16). In some instances, angelic beings are said to be ministers of God's will (Ps. 103:19-22; cf. Is. 6:1-7), but their intermediary role does not diminish nature's continual dependence on Yahweh's ultimate personal rule.

One important implication of this approach is that there are no "laws of nature" in the popular modern sense, that is, immanent forces forming an unbreakable causal chain of occurrences and making nature function as a perpetual motion machine. Concomitantly, there is little support for the idea of a God who supersedes natural laws, since on the one hand there are no laws independent of him, and on the other hand, in a manner of speaking, the whole of nature is an immense constellation of Divine interventions. This, in turn, means that the Old Testament approach to miracles differs from the view that a miracle is supernatural or even contrary to nature. Of two typical Old Testament "miracles," the crossing of the Jordan under Joshua and the child-bearing of Sarah in advanced years, H. Wheeler Robinson has remarked: "Those are to be regarded as extensions of the Divine power which is being constantly exercised in more normal occurrences–the wonders of the deep, the mysteries of childbirth." Miracles, in other words, are "representative occasions" when the Divine activity "specially impresses human consciousness." [29]

In the New Testament the emphasis on the present rule of God takes a characteristic christological form, for the most part. Faced with the predicament that the Kingdom of God did not dawn precisely as Jesus had said it would,[30] the early Church did not abandon the hope that the Kingdom would come eventually (cf. e.g., Gal. 5:21), but postulated an interim period when the enthroned Messiah rules with God.[31] The Father, the Church believed, has given all things to the Son (Mt. 11:27; Jn. 3:35; 13:3; I Cor. 15:27; Eph. 1:22) and, at the end, the Son will return the Kingdom to the Father (I Cor. 15:28). In the meantime Christ reigns over all things as exalted Lord.[32]

For the New Testament as for the Old, there are no immanent, autonomous or quasi-autonomous "laws of Nature" (or their equivalent) with which God must contend.[33] God rules immediately throughout his creation (cf. Acts 17:27f.; Eph. 4:6). Sparrows fall by his will (Mt. 10:29). He sends the fruitful rains (Mt. 5:45; Acts 14:17). He feeds the birds of the air and clothes the grass with lilies (Mt. 6:26, 30). He gives life to all things (I Tim. 6:13). In a manner reminiscent of Yahweh's redemptive power in the Exodus events, the Son exercises sovereign authority over the world of nature: "And he awoke and rebuked the wind, and said to the sea, 'Peace! Be still!' And the wind ceased, and there was a great calm" (Mk. 4:39). Jesus also walks on the sea (Mk. 6:45-52), curses a fig tree (Mk. 11:12-14, 20), multiplies bread (Mk. 6:34-44; 8:1-9), and changes water into wine (Jn. 2:1-11). All these mighty works (with the possible exception of the last) should be viewed as "miracles" in the Old Testament sense, that is, wondrous events exhibiting and extending God's creative rule, not isolated suspensions of immutable laws of nature.[33]

If, however, the whole of nature is at every moment a pliant instrument in the hands of God, if it can be said that "all things are thy servants" (Ps. 119:91) and "all things are possible with God" (Mk. 10:27), this does not mean that nature is without *order*. That it could only be if its God were not deliberate. But God's creation by speaking is a purposeful act [34] that gives the natural world a certain structure. This is indicated especially by the Priestly writer. As Edmund Jacob has stated: "The author of the Priestly creation narrative shows God setting the elements in order like an architect intending to build a house." [35] The idea of nature as a house solidly built is expended by the poetic parallel to the Priestly account, Psalm 104,[36] where nature is a work of art with a harmonious order.[37] The idea of nature as a structured whole is also found elsewhere in the Old Testament. "The comparison with a house," Jacob explains, "which is only hinted at by the Priestly author, is explicitly developed in the Book of Job (38:4-7) where all the acts of the architect are attributed to God: marking off of the land, laying of the foundation and the corner stone." [38] The image of a creative speaking by God led naturally to the complementary idea of his creative wisdom:

It is he who made the earth by his power,
who established the world by his wisdom,
and by his understanding stretched out the heavens,
When he utters his voice there is a tumult of waters in the heavens,
and he makes the mist rise from the ends of the earth.
(Jer. 12:12-13a; cf. Job 28:23-27; Ps. 104:24)

And in the classic statement:

Ages ago I [wisdom] was set up
* * *
When he established the heavens, I was there,
* * *
when he marked out the foundations of the earth,
then I was beside him, like a master workman.
(Pr. 8:23-30; cf. 3:19)

Yahweh "did not create it a chaos; he formed it to be inhabited" (Is. 45:18), that is, to be a place of peaceful order. So Yahweh gives the sun for light by day and fixes the order of the moon and stars for light by night (Jer. 31:35; cf. Job. 38:33). So he appoints the time for harvest (Jer. 5:24). Yahweh has made a covenant with the earth (Gen. 9:13; Jer. 33:20, 25) to which he is faithful:

> For ever, O Lord, thy word is
> firmly fixed in the heavens.
> Thy faithfulness endures to all generations;
> thou hast established the earth and it stands fast.
> By thy appointment they stand this day.
> (Ps. 119:89-91a)

In a certain sense, then, nature does have a law, but this law is not a permanently fixed, self-sufficient, immanent force, it is the faithful and powerful presence of God working within his domain, directing it toward his Final Future.

V. A New Horizon: The Kingdom of God

G. K. Chesterton tells the story of a man who set sail from England to explore the world. After many bouts with the sea, and days and nights sailing through foggy weather, the voyager finally sighted land. With great relief he strode ashore and planted his feet firmly on English soil.

The biblical approach to nature has been under our feet all these years! But it has taken a long journey to discover it. Now, with a fairly good idea of where we are, how can we build a theological home on this "new" territory?

1. The American Dilemma and the Biblical Vision

As far as the American theme Civilization versus Nature is concerned, we are on fruitful soil. We have biblical authority to counteract the immensely influential, but thoroughly one-sided Protestant notion that the only *raison d'être* of nature is the being and well-being of man.[1] From the biblical point of view nature has its own integrity in the eyes of God, a value and meaning not exhausted by what it does and signifies for man. Having its own role of play in the universal Divine drama of creation, redemption, and consummation, nature therefore has its own rights before man.

The closely related Puritan and capitalistic emphases on man's dominion over nature can now be seen to be equally one-sided. As far as the Bible is concerned, and man is viewed as being worth more than nature in God's eyes (Mt. 7:26) and is given dominion over nature and in that sense the Bible allows, and even encourages, a utilitarian relation between man and nature. But the Bible consciously limits the utilitarian relationship, and envisions respect, at times even delight, on all sides of the relation.

Nor does the Bible present us with nature pictured as a self-driven machine occasionally interrupted by interventions of Divine power. The biblical approach thus stands over against the mechanical model which has so consistently buttressed the Western exploitative approach. Nature is not a self-enclosed machine but an immense constellation of God's activity, an ocean of Divine power and wisdom, constantly in flux under his guidance.

So the biblical approach, properly understood, can only have the effect of radically relativizing the American theme Civilization versus Nature. Concerning the other theme, Nature versus Civilization, little needs to be said. The biblical writers are intensely concerned about social justice in the city of man. The same prophet who proclaims the renewal of nature, who imagines the wolf and the lamb lying down together, consistently says to the people of Israel, "What do you mean by crushing my people, by grinding the face of the poor?" Jesus concluded the very discourse in which he invited his hearers to consider the lilies of the field by urging his audience to seek first the Kingdom of God and his righteousness. This motif is carried to the very end in II Peter: "We wait for a new heaven and a new earth in which righteousness dwells" (II Peter 3:15). The seer of the Book of Revelation looks forward not only to a new heaven and a new earth but also to a renewed city of man, a new Jerusalem (Rev. 21:2).

There is no basis in the Bible, then, for the romantic flight from social reality to the wilderness, notwithstanding the role "the wilderness theme" has played in both biblical and American history. The Bible affirms the rights of civilization no less—indeed more—than the rights of nature. In particular, the polemic of the Old Testament against the religions of Canaan was directed against their rigid and iniquitous social conservatism, which was defended in the name of the gods of nature (see, for example, Isaiah 57). Thus biblical thought stands over against the obsessive American drama with nature, opposing both themes—Nature versus Civilization as well as Civilization versus Nature.

2. Rudiments for a Theology of Nature: the Kingdom of God as Creative Rule and Created Realm

It is one thing to know where one stands, on good soil with a high productive potential; it is another to harvest real fruits from that soil. Merely to identify the biblical approach to nature is not enough. We must appropriate its potential *in our own terms,* if we are to respond fruitfully to the problems of our own time. This means that we must plant the tree of theological reflection in the biblical soil. There is no permanent short-cut from that soil to the ecological good works we so desperately need today. Surely, biblical insights can prod and inspire us directly, from time to time. But they also can be quickly discounted in the name of modernity. We must therefore accept the responsibility and the risk of saying in our own words to our community of faith what the biblical writers said in their time to their community of faith. This procedure will not guarantee all the ecological fruits we need, but at least *in principle* it will allow the claims of biblical faith to be heard *as claims* in our day and not as mere gleanings from the ancient world to take or leave as we please.

But we need the right kind of seed if the theological tree is to take root; we need a fundamental theological intuition, or model, suited to the biblical way of thinking. We need an imaginative framework which will hold our thoughts together in a way that allows them to correspond to the biblical mind. The fundamental theological intuition which seems to be best suited to biblical thinking is a motif from the Bible itself—*the Kingdom of God.*

This theme commends itself for two major reasons. First, it opens our reflection in a thoroughgoing way, at least in principle, to a social ethic which emphasizes justice in the city of man. It is no accident that the theology of Walter Rauschenbusch, and behind that the theology of sectarian Calvinism, gave a key place to the image of the Kingdom of God in their emphasis on a social gospel. One can also recall that the call of the prophets for social justice emerged in a theological context dominated by the image of a Divine Monarchy. This is not to suggest that the employment of that image guarantees an ethic geared to social justice. But given the conservative social ideology traditionally associated with concern for nature, our theological reflection should be built on a foundation that encourages rather than discourages an ethic of social change and justice.

Second, the image of the Kingdom of God makes it possible for us to avoid the kind of problematic personalism which has come to dominate contemporary theology, at least in Protestantism. Karl Barth and Emil Brunner, for example, give direct theological attention exclusively to the Divine history with man, as we already have had occasion to observe. The corollary of this focus is that nature is merely the scenery for that history, with the result that the biblical approach to nature is obscured rather than illuminated.[2]

Employing the theme of the Kingdom of God as a germinative conceptual framework, then, can help us to steer clear of both the narrow personalism of theologians like Barth and Brunner and the so-called hyper-personalism of theologians like Tillich. It allows us to conceive of a personal God who relates himself directly both to a personal creature (man) and to an a-personal creature (the whole of nature) with the same degree of intensity, if not the same kind of intimacy. This, in principle, will allow us to do justice to the Bible's picture of the Divine history with nature. At the same time, it is evident that the image preserves and emphasizes the personalism of the biblical vision: a king is fittingly thought of as one who deliberates, acts, enjoys, loves, punishes, and generally relates himself to both things and people in a personal way.

But if it is to allow us to highlight the Divine history with nature, the image must be carefully qualified. For, at least since the time of Immanuel Kant, the connotation of the image has been dominantly spiritual.[3] "The Kingdom of God" has generally referred to the ethical relations between a monarch and a community of self-conscious subjects, and/or to the ethical relations within that community. Kant used the picture of a Divine Kingdom to refer chiefly to an "ethical commonwealth" or a "people of God under ethical laws." [4] This spiritualizing employment of the image is not altogether different from that of Augustine, who identified the Kingdom with the Church, understood as a community of people belonging both to the present age and to the final, eschatological age.[5] Similar ideas can be found in the New Testament—for example, in the Book of Revelation.[6] The image will be employed here however, in a more comprehensive way.

A king's dominion extends not only to his human subjects,

but to all his geographical territory as well. He commands that a building or a road be built or that a forest be cleared, and it is done. Physical territory is essential for an established kingdom, and the king controls that territory. He can enter, as it were, into a deliberate and sustained relationship with his physical domain. This is to suggest that the king can plan how he will act in relation to his physical territory over an extended period and can set his final goal for that territory.[7] He can take action from day to day, from year to year, to implement his long-range plan. The king can also take joy in his work in relation to his physical territory. If he takes action along such lines, the king will be entering into a *history* with his physical territory. This is *not* to suggest that the territory somehow must be a *conscious* participant in the sustained relation with the king. But the relation is mutual insofar as the various constituents of his physical domain react to the king's activity.[8] Moreover, the king can respond to the reactions occasioned by his initial activity. At the end of his reign, perhaps, the ruler may choose to write an account of his sustained relation to his physical territory and this could properly be called a history.

In such a manner the metaphor of the Kingdom of God can be so conceived as to comprehend the whole natural world. We thus have a personalistic conceptual framework which allows us to do justice to that biblical picture of a Divine history with nature.

The broader conception of the Kingdom of God, it is instructive to note, is characteristic of the theology of Luther and Calvin. It is evident in Luther's "Two Kingdoms" doctrine: the first Kingdom is the sphere of the Creator's dynamic rule over the whole of his creation, over all nature as well as world-history.[9] Calvin, in his own way, also conceives of the Kingdom as extending to the whole of nature.[10] A similar use of the image is also found in both the New and the Old Testaments. As we have seen Jesus' proclamation of the Kingdom of God includes the idea of a final *world*-transformation. The Book of Revelation envisions the *world* as having become the Kingdom of God and his Christ (11:15) with the implicit idea of the creation of a new heaven and a new earth (cf. 21:1), along with the implicit idea of a more spiritual kingdom, the New Jerusalem (cf. 21:2). In the Old Testament the theme of the world-encompassing rule of God is also strongly represented, as for example in the prayer of David in I Chronicles 29:11.

So the Kingdom of God is comprehensive, including the world of nature no less than the world of man. The image also refers distinctively to the *creative working* of God, on the one hand, and his *created works* on the other. It refers to a Divine *rule* and to a Divine *realm.* The first idea points primarily to activity by the sovereign; the second primarily to the sphere governed by the sovereign. This double connotation expresses the fundamental biblical conviction that God both *rules majestically* throughout his creation and rules majestically throughout his *creation.* The biblical writers take seriously both the government of God and the world in which his rule holds sway.

We must strive to hold both notions, rule and realm, in balance. If the rule is too much emphasized, the realm may appear a mere extension of the rule, the creation no more than an extension of the Creator. The King would then have no real domain, and would *de facto* be no King, unless one can somehow conceive of a King who rules over himself alone. If, on the other hand, the realm is too much emphasized, the rule may appear dispensable and the realm autonomous. But a kingdom without a King has ceased *de facto* to be a kingdom. Both extremes therefore, rule-without-realm and realm-without-rule, should be avoided. The biblical writers know neither a

Creator who is indistinguishable from his creation, nor a creation which is autonomous.[11]

With these rudiments for a theology of nature in hand, with these theological seeds, we can now venture to till the soil of biblical faith; first with some concrete statements about the creative rule of God, then some observations concerning the created realm of God.

VI. The Creative Rule of God

A certain Rembrandt etching shows three trees at the edge of a knoll, with the field below darkened by shadows and the sky above turbulent with cumulus clouds. The etching seems to vibrate with motion, almost as if the hand of the artist were somehow drawing in each line as you watch. Imagine now that that pulsating landscape is the universe, and that the hands of the artist are the hands of God. Call this etching the Kingdom of God.

First we will focus our attention on the work of the *artist,* the *creative rule* of God, then on the *work* of the artist, his *created realm.* As we consider the first aspect of the Kingdom, we will be exploring nature's own integrity in the eyes of God. As we consider the second, we will move toward an understanding that nature and civilization are fellow citizens.

1. The Divine History with Nature

The creative rule of God is not static. We will consider presently the ways in which God powerfully establishes all things, wisely shapes all things, and joyfully values all things. But these three moments of his creative rule are not somehow timeless. Although they do not follow one another sequentially, but in fact are simultaneous aspects of God's rule, they are nevertheless moments in process, moments on the way. When God establishes, shapes, and values all things, he always does so with a goal in mind, the new creation of all things, the consummation of his own creative rule.

The final goal of all things is the glorious Divine sabbath rest, the finally fulfilled time, when God will be all in all. This goal determines and defines all the other works: The establishing power of God is purposeful power; like a river which flows to the ocean, it ever moves toward its Final Rest. His wise shaping of the universe is temporally as well as spatially oriented; all things are suited to each other not only so as to be orderly and beautiful now, but so as to one day break forth in the glorious concert of the Last Day. The joyous valuing by God of all things is not only related to things as they are now, but to things as they will be. In a word, the creative rule of God is not only the ever-present Alpha of the universe, it is the coming Omega as well.

This is to restate and to develop a number of biblical motifs. Creation for the Priestly writer means that the way is being prepared for a final saving good, with the Divine Rest functioning as a kind of *telos*.[1] For Deutero-Isaiah and his school, Yahweh is not only the First, who laid the foundations of the earth, but the Last, who will usher in the new heavens and the new earth. We have noted a similar theme in the teaching of Jesus, his proclamation of the Kingdom of God as the coming world-transformation. Paul, who confessed the eternal power and glory of God in the things that have been made (Ro. 1:20), also looked toward their final transformation on the day when all things would finally be God's (I Cor. 15:28; cf. Ro. 11:36), when "the creation itself will be set free from its bondage to decay and obtain the glorious liberty of the children of God" (Ro. 8:21). This theme is summed up in the Apocalypse's reaffirmation of Deutero-Isaiah's proclamation of the new heavens and the new earth (Rev. 21:1).

The theme that the Last Day will be a day for the whole of nature, not just for humanity, has often been neglected in Western theology, particularly in the Augustinian tradition with its preoccupation with the *City* of God. This tradition seems to have found a contemporary and influential spokesman in Teilhard de Chardin. Teilhard conceives of the history of the universe as the development of greater and greater complexity and consciousness in a progression toward a final *Omega-point.* In this concept of a final fulfillment he appears to mean Christ alone, together with the transfigured Body of believers. Teilhard apparently holds that the extra-human world of nature will be left behind on the Last Day of christic-human consummation.[2] If that is Teilhard's doctrine, it is inadequate. The biblical affirmation is not only of the coming City of God, but of the coming new heavens and new earth as well (cf. Rev. 21; also II Peter 3:13). The concept of the telos of the world being the *Omega-point* fails to convey the fulness of biblical eschatology and can only have the effect of undercutting essential elements in a theology of nature. For, if the whole of nature (with the possible exception of human corporality) is to fall away into nothingness, that means it has no ultimate worth. The whole of nature would have to be treated, then, as merely a backdrop for the Divine history with man. The integrity of nature, its role as a participant in its own right in the universal Divine drama of creation, redemption, and consummation, would be demolished. It would be much more adequate to speak of the *Omega-world* as the telos of the universe. At the same time, to appropriate Teilhard's concept of the development of complexity-consciousness, we might speak of a *point* of *Divine intimacy* within the *Omega-world,* which would represent the consummation of the process of complexity-consciousness. This would be the transcendent City of God in the midst of the new heavens and the new earth, as the first Adam and Eve were in the midst of the first heavens and the first earth.

The theology of nature thus necessarily extends into the theology of last things. Yet as we enter this province we should recognize that our theological language must remain, when all has been said, the language of prayer. It is salutary to recall here the traditional saying, *omnium exeunt in mysterium.* We see, but we see through a glass darkly. We can say very little about the new creation which is more than tentative. The fact that the tree of theological reflection is not a mighty oak but a tender vine is especially evident in the present context.

Conscious of the limitations of our language and concepts, a few affirmations about the new creation may nevertheless be ventured. First, two formal statements. The new creation will stand in a relation of *continuity* with the first creation. The creative rule of God will not destroy the first creation and establish something entirely different. That would be no fulfillment. "For the substance of the creation is not annihilated, since he who established it is faithful. Rather the form of the world passes away," said Irenaeus.[3] At the same time, however, the new creation will stand in a relation of *radical transcendence* to the first (cf. II Peter 3:12f.). The Last Day of the Divine Rest will not be "more of the same."

Secondly, the new creation will be the end of the "dark side" of the first creation. All the chaotic elements of nature will be put to rest. This seems to be the meaning of the Apocalypse's affirmation that the sea will be no more (Rev. 21:1). The natural pain and death of the first creation will thereby be overcome (Rev. 21:4).[4] So too, aggression and conflict of the first creation will vanish in the "peaceable kingdom."

The wolf shall dwell with the lamb, and the leopard shall lie down with the kid, and the calf and the lion and the fatling together; and the lion shall eat straw like the ox. The sucking child shall play over the hole of the asp, and the weaned child shall put his hand on the adder's den. (Is. 11:6-8)

The wildness will remain, to be sure, for God also loves the alligators and the mountain lions and wills their fulfillment. But the dream of a wilderness without darkness and violence and pain will come true. That is the visionary confession which biblical faith encourages: When the saints go marching in, "night shall be no more; they need no light of lamp or sun, for the Lord God will be their light, and they shall reign for ever and ever" (Rev. 22:5). This goal of the creative rule of God, this Final Future, informs God's powerful establishing of all things, his wise shaping of all things, and his joyous valuing of all things. The present creation will give way to the new.

But the history of God with nature also comprehends the movement of the present creation within its own sphere. We can speak (cautiously) here of the *cosmic epochs* of God's history with nature. This is to restate and develop the Priestly conception of a deliberate, temporal unfolding of the creative work of God. (Whether these cosmic epochs are seven in number is an unimportant question which reflects a literalistic interpretation of the Priestly creation narrative.)

Further, it is possible to speak—especially with reference to the theme of the Divine wisdom—of an orderly development from one cosmic epoch to another. Here, however, the theologian is not permitted to introduce the concept of evolution for he does not have the data in his primary source, the biblical witness, which would allow him to speak in any technical sense about such a process in nature. On the other hand, the scientific doctrine of evolution surely complements and is complemented by the theological idea of cosmic epochs. Nothing in this notion contradicts the idea of vast stretches of cosmic time prior to the appearance of man, during which a highly complex process of evolution was occurring. In one of his essays, Bertrand Russell once asked: If God was so interested in man, why did He take so long in creating him? "What was the point of the ichthyosaurs, diplodochi, mastodons, and so on?" [5] To this kind of question, one can respond that God was indeed profoundly interested in man from the very beginning, but not only man. He was also deeply interested in the ichthyosaurs and the dinosaurs and even the primordial slime from which life first emerged. The Divine purpose is profoundly cosmocentric, as well as anthropocentric. God rules majestically and joyously over the eons as well as over the history of mankind.

If the course of the universe proceeds through cosmic epochs, can we say when these epochs will end? The answer is No. With regard to last things (eschatology), as with regard to first things (protology), caution ought to be the rule in theology. The "heat death" of the universe forecast by at least a few natural scientists may somehow be a prelude to the new creation, just as the "big bang" beginning of the universe described by some physicists could have been the aftermath of the initial moment of God's creative activity. But it is quite conceivable that both the first and final stages of the universe, as they are now envisioned in the natural sciences, encompass only some of the Divinely created cosmic epochs. The first things and the last are hidden in the mind and heart of God.

In a certain sense, finally, where we are in the history of cosmic epochs *is not even known by God.* This touches on a highly complicated theological problem, which is receiving more and more attention today, especially by those theologians influenced by Whitehead—the problem of the Divine foreknowledge. Does God know the future, and if so in what sense? As

Charles Hartshorne and others have pointed out, one abstract or speculative concept which has played an influential role in Christian theology is of the God projected analogically by the *via negativa.*[6] The *via negativa* leads us to notice, for example, that man's knowledge is imperfect: God's knowledge, in contrast, must therefore be perfect. So, it is thought, God must have an intricate knowledge of the future course of nature. Nature must be spread before him as an open book, while we men have yet to turn the pages.

An extra-biblical notion of absoluteness, inconsistent with biblical personalism, has played a role here. Absoluteness is conceived as impassibility: God does not change. If there is something that God does not know now (in this case the details of the future), it is thought that one day God will grow in knowledge, which will mean that he will have changed. Hence, according to this line of reasoning, the changeless God must know the future of nature as an open book. But the premise of that reasoning is faulty, for the God confessed by the biblical writers is the living God. He is a God who changes his mind on occasion (he "repents") and who responds to new developments in the history of his creatures. If God genuinely participates in that history, it is not diminishing his majesty to say he does not know all the details of the future. Indeed that lack of complete knowledge is the condition for true participation with his creatures.

God's foreknowledge of all things can easily become thought of as his predetermination of all things. *Praescientia est praedeterminatio.* The course of the universe becomes a kind of mechanical unfolding of a Divinely programmed plan. And one of the final results of this idea can only be the sapping of the vitality of our theology of nature. With an abstract absolutistic concept of God, the themes of nature as a flux and of the Divine care for and responsiveness to nature, both of which are crucial for the theology of nature, will eventually be excluded, since all things would have to be seen as following each other by virtual necessity.

We can say, surely, that God knows what *has been* and what *is*. He also knows surely, *what his own goal for the universe is,* that is, the new creation. But, we should also say, God does not know every jot and tittle of the future. *The future is open.* The course of the cosmic epochs is not an automated exfoliation of an eternally determined plan. The present creation, the Alpha, *is*. The new creation, the Omega-world, is *not yet,* not even in eternity. The *novum* of the final creation in its fullness is still to occur. When the time is ripe, when the time is fulfilled, then God will know, and then he will usher in the new creation.[7] But not until then. And until then, God does not know how long it will be before the end time, nor exactly how and when the present constellation of nature will develop into new configurations and new stages.[8]

It will be helpful here if we recall the notion of Divine omnipotence expressed by the Reformers. Luther and Calvin maintain that his omnipotence is God's present powerful working everywhere throughout the creation. For them it is no abstract concept, not a question of what God might do or how much power he would have to have in order to carry through a variety of possibilities. Similarly, the point here is that the Divine *plan* for the universe is not an abstract map, as it were, of everything that is to happen, but *the concrete, dynamic, and all-pervasive working now* of the Divine intention to govern with power, wisdom, and joy so as to be able one day to usher in the new creation.

Here one might think of the case of a human king who has a vision for what his kingdom will someday be. If he is faithful to his goal, he will daily work, both with his lands and with his people, to shape his realm so that one day his goal will be achieved. But given the unpredictability of such variables as the climate and the human soul, he will not know now exactly when he will attain his goal. So in the greater scheme of things, the Divine King works with the spontaneity of nature [9] as well as with the freedom of history. He respects and cares for both. He will not turn either into a mere object or himself into a tyrant. As he looks to the future and acts in the present, he remains "our Father."

2. God's Powerful Establishing of Nature

Under the creative rule of God, all things are moving toward their consummation in the new creation. But the new creation does not yet exist (except in the unique case of Jesus the Messiah, considered in Chapter IX). What God is working with now is the present creation. Notwithstanding distortions to which it has been subjected (see Chapter IX), God is faithful to his original intention with regard to this created realm. In this sense, God rules as if no distortion had entered his world; he sends his rain on both the just and the unjust. He establishes, shapes, and values his created realm graciously, as from the very beginning. This is the confession of the Psalmist:

> O give thanks to the Lord, for he is good,
> for his steadfast love endures for ever . . .
> to him who alone does great wonders,
> for his steadfast love endures for ever;
> to him who by understanding made the heavens,
> for his steadfast love endures for ever;
> to him who spread out the earth upon the waters,
> for his steadfast love endures for ever.
> (Ps. 136:1, 4-6)

By his steadfast love, the Lord relates himself to the universe this very day in keeping with his original intention.

The creative rule of God can be considered first as God's powerful establishing of all things. By this I mean to depict the creative rule of God as the *immediate source* of all things. The created realm totally depends on God's activity for its being. In this connection, God has sometimes been referred to as the "fountain" of all things: [10] Luther pictures God as being "with all creatures, flowing, and pouring into them, filling all things." [11]

The creative rule of God, moreover, is the source of the world with respect to *individuals* within it as well as the whole. God establishes a galaxy as well as the universe, a planet as well as the solar system, and, closer to the microscopic realm, a blade of grass or a photon as well as a field or an atom. As Calvin remarks, "It is certain that not one drop of rain falls without God's sure command." [12]

To this, however, we must add two important qualifications. The first is required by the somewhat impersonal or a-personal force of the image "source," which by itself might be taken to suggest a rule somehow blind, arbitrary, or insensitive. But the King of the universe confessed by the biblical writers, and especially by Jesus, exercises a paternal government. He is Our Father, responsive to all his creatures–"These all look to thee, to give them their food in due season" (Ps. 104:27). As Calvin says, God "exercises special care over each of his works." He is Creator, Governor, and Preserver "not only in that he drives the celestial frame as well as its several parts by a universal motion, but also in that he sustains, nourishes, and cares for, everything he has made, even to the least sparrow." [13] Luther makes the same point in commenting on Hebrews 1:3, concerning God's *upholding* all things: "This word captures the idea of a certain delightful care we might say. The idea is found in Deuteronomy 32:11, 'He spread out his wings and took him up, and carried him on his back.' " [14] The creative rule of God as the source of all things is thus personal, caring, and sensitive. The King of the universe watches over all his works with paternal concern, no matter how insignificant any individual work may appear to be.

It is evident that with this idea, secondly, we are at the limit of the powers of human conceptualization. It is truly difficult to conceive what Calvin means when he says that not one drop of rain can fall without God's sure command. For the only conceptual model we have to work with is the finite human self with its finite consciousness. *We* can be conscious of just so many things at one time; hence we can issue only a finite number of "commands." How could God possibly care for all the galaxies and all the electrons? This *how* does not seem to admit of an answer except again the traditional *omnia exeunt in mysterium.* The majesty of the Divine rule dwarfs our ways and our thoughts: "For as the heavens are higher than the earth, so are my ways higher than your ways and my thoughts than your thoughts" (Is. 55:9). God is "King of kings and Lord of lords, who alone has immortality and dwells in unapproachable light, whom no man has ever seen or can see" (I Tim. 6:15). Again at this point, in other words, theological language can only be what it always is, the language of prayer.

The problem of the individual is not, however, a concern just for the theology of nature. We meet a similar configuration of questions in the theology of history. How can God govern more than a billion people on this planet (and perhaps others on other planets)? So too for the theology of piety: how can my personal communion with God make any difference to him?—since I am only one little voice among so many others. How can God attend to a single group or person? How can he remember me when I die? These questions press our finite imagination to the breaking point. Notwithstanding the inadequacy of our concepts, however, our confession must be that God *does indeed* attend to even the most insignificant of individuals—"But even the hairs of your head are numbered" (Mt. 10:30). *How* God does this is not finally within our power to say. The creative Source of our universe is clothed in mystery.

The creative rule of God in its moment of powerful establishing is also the *continuing* source of all that is.[15] Luther reminds us "how incessantly active God is in all his creatures, allowing none of them to take a holiday."[16] The world is totally dependent not only for its being, but also for its becoming. In no sense, and at no time, is it a self-sufficient, self-enclosed whole. Concomitantly, there are no immanent "laws of nature" which stand apart from the creative rule of God, by which that rule is somehow limited.[17] God did not set the world in motion, step back, and then recognize that the turning of its wheels and cogs was a *fait accompli* which must be accepted as is, or be interrupted in emergencies by an exercise of extraordinary power. The unity and the course of nature are established by the creative rule of the heavenly King. Nature does not hold itself together, nor does it advance to new constellations of being by itself.[18]

One might summarize by saying that each natural occurrence and the whole world of nature is a Divine wonder. Every entity and the whole magnificent system is the result of concentrated Divine action. As Luther says, a single grain of wheat is full of "many miraculous works." Of the whole world in relation to the mystery of the Eucharist he comments: "If it were possible and I should measure all creatures and describe them in words, you would see wonders just as great, nay, even greater, than in this sacrament."[19] The sharpness of this conception perhaps comes out best when it is set in historical context.

The accent in Luther and Calvin is on the immediacy of God and his continuing activity in, with, and under *all* things. One cannot hold that God is *more* immediate, let us say, to an animal than he is to a stone, or to a man than to an animal. In contrast, Augustine holds to the idea of a hierarchy of being extending from God through the angels, man, animals, plants to the material elements, and ultimately to non-being. According to this view, God's governance is more directly exercised in the higher than the lower segments of the chain of being. Here is Augustine in his treatise on the Trinity:

The will of God, which makes his angels and his ministers a burning fire (Ps. 103:4), presiding among spirits which are joined together in perfect peace and amity, and kindled into one will by a kind of spiritual charity, seated as it were on an exalted, holy, secret throne, as in its own house and its own temple, thence diffuses itself through all things by certain perfectly ordered movements of created things, firstly spiritual, then corporeal. . . . As the more gross and inferior bodies are governed in a certain order by the more subtle and powerful ones, so too all bodies are governed by the living spirit, the irrational living spirit that makes default and sins by the living and rational spirit that is pious and just, and the last by God himself, and thus the whole creation by its Creator.[20]

A similar complex of ideas is found in the thought of Thomas Aquinas—with the difference that under the influence of Aristotelian metaphysics the hierarchical structure of the world is a more fixed, self-enclosed structure than in the thought of Augustine.[21] Interestingly, it was in the twelfth century that, under the influence of Aristotelian metaphysics, an increasing emphasis was laid on the idea that every miracle somehow superseded the laws of nature by the exercise of Divine power. In the thirteenth century, following this trend, Thomas himself so defines miracle that "the essential and almost exclusive note was the transcendence of all created forces by the intervention of God's omnipotence." [22] Behind this supranaturalistic understanding of miracle stands the tendency to allow the idea of the omniactivity of God to coalesce with the idea of a fixed order of being. In the face of such a development, a genuine act of God had to be conceived of as setting aside a fixed finite order.

In contrast to Augustine and Aquinas, the Reformers reject the idea of a hierarchy of being with descending levels of mediating agents between God and nature. They conceive God as immediately and constantly present to the whole of nature as to other aspects of his creation. As Luther writes,

> It is God who creates, effects, and preserves all things through his almighty power and righthand, as our Creed confesses. *For he dispatches no officials or angels when he creates or preserves something, but all this is the work of the Divine power itself.* If he is to create or preserve it, however, he must be present and must make and preserve his creation both in its innermost and outermost aspects.[23]

Commenting on Psalm 115:3 ("Our God is in heaven, he does what he pleases"), Calvin writes, perhaps with direct reference to the Thomistic view: "It would be senseless to interpret the words of the prophet after the manner of the philosophers, that God is the first agent because he is the beginning and cause of all motion." No, "a certain deliberate will is meant." God's governance can hardly be enclosed "within the stream of nature . . . as though he allowed all things by a free course to be borne along according to a universal law of nature." God is not one who "sometimes ceases and sits in idleness, or continues by a general impulse that order of nature which he previously appointed." Rather, "he so regulates all things that nothing takes place without his deliberation." [24]

In retrospect, what Augustine and Thomas did was to emphasize the notion of the Divine realm at the expense of the Divine rule. Luther and Calvin, on the other hand, took the notion of a creative Divine rule with persistent seriousness, not allowing it to be identified with the realm of God. This explains why their theologies are so helpful for our reflection about the meaning of the biblical view of nature. For the biblical writers take the Kingdom of God as *rule* with utmost seriousness. There is no noticeable tendency in the Bible to allow the rule to coalesce with the realm of God and to view the latter as in any sense autonomous.

If, with Luther and Calvin, we say that nature, considered as a whole and as a congregation of individuals, is one immense constellation of Divine activity, then every event and complex of events can be said to have an intrinsically wondrous character.[25] Nature is an ocean of wondrous events, for God powerfully establishes all things.

3. God's Wise Shaping of Nature

The creative rule of God can also be considered as his wise shaping of all things. God has fashioned the world into a concordant and beautiful structure. The master builder carefully contrives to enhance the inner coherence and beauty of the building he is constructing while he is at work. This image is employed in the Old Testament, where the created world is thought of as constructed in wisdom (Ps. 104:24) to display a "wonderful properness and harmony" (the apparent meaning of "very good" in Genesis 1:31).[26]

God's shaping of the world as a *concordant whole* is brought out strikingly in the First Letter of Clement to the Corinthians (ca. 95 A.D.):

> The heavens are moved by his management and obey him in peace. Day and night pursue the course fixed by him without hindering each other. The sun and the moon and the troops of stars roll

harmoniously on their appointed courses under his direction, without any divergence from them. By his will the earth becomes fruitful and at the proper seasons produces ample food for man and beast and all the living creatures on it, without disagreement or changing any of his decisions. The unfathomable depths of the abysses and the indescribable verdicts of the underworld are held together by the same decrees. The basis of the boundless sea was gathered by his creative action into its bodies and does not go beyond the barriers surrounding it but does as he commanded it. For he said, 'Thus far you shall come and no farther, and your waves will break within you.' The ocean, impassible to man, and the worlds beyond it are regulated by the same orders from the Master. The spring, summer, autumn, and winter seasons peacefully succeed one another. The winds from their respective quarters inoffensively perform their service at the proper times. Perennial springs, created for enjoyment and health, unfailingly offer their life-giving breasts to man, and the smallest of animals get together in harmony and peace. All these things the great Creator and Master of the universe order to be in peace and harmony, in his kindness to all things. . . .[27]

Through the creative rule of God all things are held peacefully in their appointed places and blend harmoniously with one another.[28]

While God *does* shape all things for the sake of man, he also creates them for the sake of the animals, for the plants, and for the concordance of the whole. Each individual or class of individuals is wrought with a view to every other individual or class of individuals and with a view to the *gestalt*. He orders his realm so that it is not a chaos, but a cosmos.

In addition, God in his wisdom shapes the world as a *beautiful* whole. He engages himself playfully, as well as deliberately, with nature. Commenting on Proverbs 8:27-31, Hugo Rahner has observed that that passage allows us to "speak of the dancing and playing of Divine wisdom, of the child's games, when the world was made." He cites a striking statement of Gregory Nazianzen: "For the logos on high plays, stirring the whole cosmos back and forth, as he wills, into shapes of every kind." [29]

Thus the lavish colors of the birds and plants in the Amazon jungle are no accident but the result of the playfully deliberate creativity of the King of the universe [30] which was at work also on the "lilies of the fields" adorning the meadows of the Middle East. Then there is the human hand, the human face, the human body *in toto:* "The fact that Adam and Eve walked about naked was their greatest adornment before God and all creatures" says Luther.[31] Above us, moreover, are the ever glorious stars and galaxies. Within the scale of man's creative work, also, we can let our eyes rest with delight on the skyline of a New York City, on a structure like the Golden Gate Bridge, or on a waving field of sun-bathed grass. We can touch, with deep pleasure, the well-designed wood arm of a living room chair or the sensitively balanced handle of a stainless steel knife. And, with the kaleidoscopic vision of our mind's eye we can imagine something of the glories of the microscopic world, from the crystal to the surging sea of sub-atomic particles. As Calvin exclaims, "You cannot in one glance survey this most vast and beautiful system of the universe, in its wide expanse, without being completely overwhelmed by the boundless force of its brightness." [32] All this beauty comes from the creative rule of God. It was Shelley who aptly said, "God on his throne/ Is the eldest of poets,/ Unto his measures/ Moveth the whole."

To speak of God's beautifying all things in this way is not to suggest that all things are necessarily shaped to be congenial to man in every respect. Indeed, one can say that God in his wisdom introduces into nature elements *alien to human sensitivity* and surpassing human understanding (cf. Job 28:13, 23; Is. 55:9). This is implicit in the Psalmist's statement that the *night* is made for the wild beasts, wherein they may seek and devour their prey (Ps. 104:20f.; cf. Job 38:39f.). So too, the hawk and the eagle soar by Divine wisdom, the eagle bringing prey to his nest where "his young ones suck up blood" (Job 39:26-30). God even provides a place for the horrendous Leviathans of the deep (cf. Ps. 104:26; Job 41). The powerful poem of William Blake moves even the man who has only rested his eyes for a moment or two on a tiger in a zoo:

> Tiger! Tiger! burning bright
> In the forests of the night,
> What immortal hand or eye
> Could frame thy fearful symmetry?
>
> In what distant deeps or skies
> Burnt the fire of thine eyes?
> On what wings dare he aspire?
> What the hand dare seize the fire?
>
> And what shoulder, and what art,
> Could twist the sinews of thy heart?
> And when thy heart began to beat,
> What dread hand? and what dread feet?
>
> What the hammer? what the chain?
> In what furnace was thy brain?
> What the anvil? what dread grasp
> Dare its deadly terrors clasp?

The luminaries of our skies, if we were near them or if they were to come near to us, would be more horrible to us than a caldron of molten steel. Yet every star is ordained by God's wisdom and has a certain dreadful sublimity, as well as that beauty which is more congenial to us. Some of the technological Leviathans of our day—the massive quasi-autonomous computers, the monstrous bulldozers, the vast automated factories, the gigantic military cargo planes, the laser beam, the thermonuclear reaction—are shaped in wisdom by the creative rule of God albeit through the minds and hands of men.

One cannot discuss God's wise shaping of the world as a

concordant and beautiful whole, however, without saying something explicit about the problem of sin, death, disease, and suffering. Sin is not a harmonious element in a concordant whole, but a discordant note introduced *against* the rule of God. We can properly say that God works with sinful man, externally as it were, thereby drawing his sinful activity into a certain order. But we should not say that God effects or creates man's sin, for there is no biblical evidence for that.

The notion that sin is fundamentally discord qualifies our understanding of the beauty of human life in God's created realm. The dreadful beauty of a pride of hunting lions, or a thermo-nuclear explosion on the sun, or a gigantic computer in a medical lab is different from that of a well-disciplined line of soldiers marching off to war, or a thermo-nuclear explosion in a Hiroshima, or a computer used to run a factory producing napalm. Human sin has the effect of transforming the intrinsically beautiful into the extrinsically ugly. This is even true of some of man's most cherished objects of beauty. Berthold Brecht once commented that when he saw a placid, picturesque, idyllic fishing village, he noticed first the torn fishing nets. The sensitive onlooker will never forget that the majestic pyramids were built by slave labor or that the beauty of the New York skyline cloaks the tormented ghetto of Harlem. The ugly reality of man's sin taints the beautiful creations wrought by his hands. When the goodness of God's created realm is distorted, in other words, its beauty is distorted too. To say this is only to scratch the surface of the problem of the relationship of human sinfulness to the beautifying aspect of the Divine rule, but it is enough to show the direction in which a more lengthy discussion could fruitfully proceed.

We touch on an equally complex problem when we consider the question whether death, disease, and physical suffering in general belong to the realities established by the Creator-King, or whether they are intrusions occasioned by sin. Even to raise this question is to stand at a certain distance from the main line of theological tradition, for many theologians have assumed or explicitly taught that physical death is the result of sin.[33] Nevertheless it is possible to contend that both death and suffering belong in some sense to the world as created. Such modern theologians as Reinhold Niebuhr, Paul Althaus, and Karl Barth have argued persuasively in this vein.[34] The theology of the Bible generally seems to move in the same direction,[35] providing little support for the alternative view that physical death and suffering are the result of a cosmic fall.[36] To be sure, this problem merits further study. But the way to a doctrine that physical death and suffering belong to the creation *qua* creation seems open, notwithstanding its divergence from the main course of the theological tradition. We will return to this topic in connection with a consideration of pain and death in relation to human sinfulness.

Still, one question arises at this point which should be answered before we proceed further. How does this view of suffering and physical death as intrinsic features of the created realm affect our understanding of the goodness of creation? First, the teaching of both the Bible and the theological tradition generally is that God created the world *good, not perfect.* This essentially good world is still to be consummated in the perfect world that is to come. Second, the "dark side" of the created realm refers to elements alien to human sensitivity, from the molten core of the sun to the vicious drives of the tiger, not to elements which are intrinsically evil. In themselves the inside of the sun and the instincts of the tiger are good; they are dark only insofar as human reaction is concerned. To speak metaphorically: Before the fall Adam lived in harmony with the sun and the tiger because he was a man of faith and therefore knew the proper limits of his relationship to these creatures. He did not try to fly like Icarus to the sun, nor to live like Tarzan in the territory of the tiger. Adam kept a certain distance from these and other fellow creatures. It was only after his fall that he tried to claim the territory of the sun and the tiger as his own. And *then* those elements which were only alien to his sensitivity became actually destructive to his life.

Finally, the shaping moment of the creative rule of God is not exhausted in relation to the world as a whole. God also shapes the world as a *constellation of concordant and beautiful individuals*. He makes a particular maple tree, for example; he does not merely structure "treehood." [37] Similarly, and as wondrously, the King of all things arranges the being of every snowflake.[38] In like manner he sculpts the human face and fixes the lines of the hand and fingers. Individuality, we may say, has eternal meaning in and through the creative rule of God. This is no less true of those individual things sculptured or designed by God through the agency of human hands—the portrait, the curtains by the window, the glass in the window, the typewriter illuminated by the light from the window. Not one of these is a nameless number, no matter if it is the result of mass production. *Sub specie aeternitatis* it has a name, a particular Divine enhancement.[39]

By the wise shaping of the creative rule of God, then, the universe is a concordant and beautiful whole constituted by concordant and beautiful individuals. Hence, "there is not a fragment in all nature, for every relative fragment of one thing is a full harmonious unity in itself. All together form the one grand palimpsest of the world" (John Muir).[40]

4. God's Joyous Valuing of Nature

We have considered the creative rule of God in two of its moments, its power and its wisdom. As power, the creative rule of God establishes all things; as wisdom, it shapes all things. From him the world has its being and becoming, on the one hand, and its order and beauty, on the other. Now we turn to consider a third moment of the creative rule of God, its joy. As joy, the creative rule of God gives value to all things and gives the world its goodness.

This theme comes into clearer focus when we recall the concrete image of God as the master builder. We can say that the master builder *takes delight* in what he has established and shaped. This, as we have seen, seems to be the significance of the Priestly writer's repeated expression in the creation narrative, "And God saw that it was good." A similar note is struck by the Psalmist in his creation-hymn: "May the Lord rejoice in his works" (Ps. 104:31b). It is also rehearsed in the wisdom literature: God's creative shaping of the world, his wisdom, "beside him like a master workman," is "daily his delight" (Pr 8:30).

But it is not immediately clear that the theme lends itself to translation into the language of value-theory. Is it meaningful to say that when God rejoices in his works he is giving value to the world? It *is* meaningful, so long as we remember that we are here concerned first of all with the creative rule of *God* and only in a secondary sense with the world. Our question, in other words, is not what is valuable within the world but what is valuable for God. We look not to what man may or may not value, but to the ultimate value-giver, to the "center of value." [41] The introduction of the technical language of value at this point will not sound so strange when we consider that the master builder, when he rejoices in the work of his hands, at the same time makes the judgment that what he has done is done *well,* that he has built at least as well as he had expected to build. So it is said: "And God saw that it was good."

Still, the central question remains unanswered: In what sense does God rejoice in all his works? In what sense does he value all things? Or to put it in slightly different form: What is the meaning of the goodness of creation?

It is instructive to note that for Karl Barth, the goodness of the created realm is its status as the external ground for the covenant of Grace. Creation is good because it is an instrument which makes possible the actualization of reconciliation and redemption. God rejoices in all things because he sees all things strictly as the preparation for the coming of Grace into the world:

> There is surely a realm of Nature [here Barth means the whole realm of creation, man together with heaven and earth] which as such is different from the realm of Grace. But at the same time in the realm of Nature *all* properties which are not directed to Grace and which do not come from Grace amount to nothing. *There is nothing in Nature which may lead a life for itself and which may follow its own course.*[42]

From the perspective of Barth's theology, the master builder must be pictured as rejoicing in his establishing and shaping only because of something *still to be added* to his work, something for which his work is the occasion or the means.

The biblical writers, however, though they conceive of creation as a stage posited by God for the sake of redemption, do not conceive it *merely* as a stage. This is indicated most succinctly perhaps by the Psalmist's hymn which celebrates God's creative works and his rejoicing in them with virtually no indication that creation is a stage for redemption (Ps. 104; cf. Ps. 29). The theology of the Bible suggests that the created realm *has value in itself for God.* Creation, to use Jonathan Edwards' terminology, is presented as an *ultimate end,* not a subordinate one. The master builder is depicted, in other words, as rejoicing in his establishing *as such* and in his shaping *as such.*[43] He values each epoch of his creative work in itself, not just as a stage on the way to the new creation.

In this respect Jonathan Edwards presents a view of creation considerably more adequate to the biblical view than Barth's. Edwards distinguishes between "original and independent ultimate ends" and "consequential and dependent ultimate ends." He then applies this distinction to the doctrine of creation:

> We must suppose that God, *before* he created the world, had some good in view as a consequence of the world's existence that was originally agreeable to him to bring the universe into existence in such a manner as he created it. But *after* the world was created, and such and such intelligent creatures actually had existence, in such and such circumstances, then a wise, just regulation of them was agreeable to God, *in itself* considered.[44]

The created realm, then, is a consequential and dependent ultimate end in which as such God rejoices.

Having considered the meaning of the Divine rejoicing with respect to the relation between creation and the new creation, we now must consider the same theme with respect to the created realm itself. Here the specific problem is the value of the natural world. Does the Creator rejoice in his works in nature *only because nature is a stage* which God posits for the sake of man, or does God rejoice in his work in nature *also because nature is for him an ultimate end?* There is little doubt that the biblical teaching, and therefore the proper theological teaching, is that nature *is* posited by God for the sake of man, that God does rejoice in nature as a means for furthering his purpose with man.[45] But is this the *only* reason why God rejoices?

Our earlier exegetical discussion has produced the clear answer that God rejoices in his work in nature as an ultimate end. God values it in itself. Recall two biblical references to animals of the deep. After God created the "great sea monsters," the Priestly author tells us in his familiar phrase that "God saw that it was good" (Gen. 1:21). That is, God delights in the sea monsters as such. He wills to have a realm in which there are such beasts for his own enjoyment. In a similar way, the Psalmist writes that God created the Leviathan in order to play with it (Ps. 104:26). God establishes and shapes a natural being without reference to the being and well-being of man. God wills to have the Leviathan for himself.

When we thrill to contemplate the almost incomprehensible reaches of our universe and try to understand that our world is more millions of years old than we can imagine, when we confront the infinitely vast spaces through which astoundingly large galaxies move or consider even the story of the evolution of life on our own planet, we may well believe that the majestic King of this universe rejoices that he has done and is doing all these works for *our* sakes.[46] For the Bible describes a God who relates himself in a special way to man and who gives the world its being so that that special relation might be established. Yet we may *also* believe, with the biblical writers, that all this temporal and spatial vastness is no mere stage or instrument posited solely for us. We may believe that the whole of nature is of intrinsic worth to God who rejoices in all his works as such. He calls the stars and planets by name (Is. 40:26; Ps. 147:7; Job 38:37), hears the cries of the animals in the wilderness (Ps. 104:27; 145:16), feeds the birds of the air (Mt. 6:26) and notices when the least sparrow falls to the ground (Lk. 12:6). He clothes the field with lilies (Mt. 6:30), and sports with the cosmic Leviathans. He wills to have the galaxies and the ichthyosaurs and the alligators and the lilies and the infinite seas of electrons, mesons, photons, and all other particles and forces for their own sakes quite apart from what they all may or may not mean for our being and well-being, as well as for the sake of our being and well-being.

In this way the King of the universe prepares all things for their transcendent Day of fulfillment, the new creation. Throughout a sequence of cosmic epochs he rules majestically in, with, and under his whole created realm. He powerfully establishes all things and so gives being and becoming to nature. He wisely shapes all things and so gives order and beauty to nature. He joyfully values all things and so gives goodness to nature. When the time comes that he judges that his finally fulfilled Omega-world can be ushered in, then he will bring his work in the present creation to an end. The creative rule of God will be consummated in the ultimate manifestation of the Divine Kingdom. Then the wolf will lie down with the lamb, and death will be no more. All things will be gloriously transformed when the day of the new heavens and a new earth dawns. The integrity of nature, its life with God, its intrinsic value in his eyes, the whole Divine history with nature, will have been vindicated.

VII. The Created Realm of God

The patron saint of modern devotees of nature is St. Francis, whose Hymn to the Sun addresses the sun and the stars and all other creatures as brothers and sisters. His visionary, sensitive appreciation of nature is unlike almost any other in Western literature. Yet Francis remains unreal. No one in his right mind would preach to the birds today. Few of even the most passionate nature-lovers truly consider the sun and the bears and the ants to be truly their brothers and sisters. The contemporary cult of the simple rustic life rarely comes close to the profound and utter sincerity of the Hymn to the Sun.

With a comprehensive theology of the Kingdom of God, however, we are in a position to salvage some–though not all of those attractive but illusive Franciscan motifs. And we can do so without accepting the cult of the simple rustic life, irresponsibly opposing the world of nature to the world of men. For we have identified an allegiance which transcends both nature and civilization. If we belong to the Kingdom of God and his righteousness, then we can no longer be primarily children of nature or primarily children of civilization. We can attend to both without opposing either one to the other. The Kingdom of God validates the rights of both nature and civilization: as subjects of the Kingdom, we are free to validate the rights of both as well.

With this new primary allegiance we can see a way to move beyond the schizophrenic American opposition between nature and civilization. To express this metaphorically, *nature and civilization are fellow citizens of the Kingdom of God.* No longer must they be intrinsically opposed, or one forgotten or neglected at the expense of the other. Each can enjoy certain inalienable rights. A man fully devoted to civilization can now call the sun and the moon and the trees his brothers and sisters.

To say that nature and civilization are fellow citizens of the Kingdom of God is to turn our attention to the Kingdom in its second aspect, not so much as the creative rule as the created realm of God. Although without his continuing rule the realm of God would have no being and becoming, no order and beauty, no goodness, the created realm does have its own distinct reality. To deny this, as we have seen, is to undercut the conceptual framework that makes it possible for us to do justice to biblical faith. A king, to be a king, must have a realm.

The created realm has two major dimensions, the natural and the human. The term dimension is used deliberately, since (unlike such a term as "sphere") it conveys both man's transcendence of and immanence in nature. Man is not immersed altogether in nature; nor is he separated from it. He exists *in* and *with* nature. The two dimensions are distinguishable but inseparable kinds of existence. We will consider the natural dimension first.

1. Nature's Life of Its Own

Nature has its own history. It lives before God in its own right. To put this more specifically, *nature has its own characteristic moments*. These moments correspond to the moments of the creative rule of God. As God powerfully establishes nature, so nature in itself has *spontaneity.* As God wisely shapes nature, so nature in itself has continuity. As God joyfully values nature, so nature in itself has congruity.

Before we consider these three created moments, the question arises whether it is meaningful to say that nature has its own moments—especially since such heavy emphasis has been laid on the creative rule of God. How can nature be totally dependent on God's rule and still have a life of its own? We must recognize clearly that we are at this point once again reaching the limits of theological understanding. Precisely how a tree can be thoroughly dependent on God's rule and still grow by itself is finally a mystery into which we cannot penetrate. This theological problem has usually been confronted directly only in the context of the discussion of *man.* Theologians have asked how one can conceive of both Divine sovereignty and human freedom without denying the reality of either one. Karl Barth has dealt with this particular problem at some length, and concludes paradoxically, "God works the creaturely working." As Barth observes, the *how* of the Creator-creature togetherness cannot be specified.[1] It seems best for us to accept a similar cognitive tension in our discussion for the present, to say simply that the creative rule of God is in, with, and under every created moment of the natural world, yet that these are not illusory, but real moments.

Spontaneity

The spontaneity of nature corresponds to its determination by the establishing power of the creative Divine rule. Nature is not locked and bound by an autonomous or quasi-autonomous chain of causality. It is not held in a rigid pattern by autonomous or quasi-autonomous "laws"—a point made earlier which bears repeating in the present context. As a whole and as a constellation of individuals, nature is open for new developments. *In this respect natural processes are more like the turbulence of a swift river than the repetitive movement of a machine.*[2] Every natural entity is open to new possibilities every moment of its existence. As a whole and as a constellation of individuals, nature continually actualizes new possibilities, moving toward new configurations of being and new patterns of becoming. The world of nature is characterized by a universal spontaneity.

Spontaneity, however, is a theological category in this context, not a natural-scientific one. The two should not be confused. Spontaneity refers to new developments such as the emergence of life on this planet. *That* there is newness in the course of nature, the theology of nature can affirm, as well as *why:* Spontaneity is real because it is established and permitted by God as the creaturely moment of correspondence to his creative rule. But *how* or *when* that spontaneity becomes evident is not for the theology of nature to specify. That is the task of the natural sciences.

In this connection two further observations are appropriate. First, the theological idea of natural spontaneity should not be confused with, or taken to entail, pan-psychism. That natural entities have, in a sense, an "inner side" which is open to the creative Divine rule can be metaphorically affirmed. That natural entities are in a certain sense self-moved can also be affirmed. But whether this "inner side" and this spontaneity are somehow *psychic* in character is a question best left to the natural sciences and to the philosophy of nature. There is no firm theological ground which allows us either to affirm or to deny a pan-psychism.[3]

The second point to be noted here concerns the relation between spontaneity and so-called "lawless" events discerned by contemporary physicists. What is spontaneous from a theological perspective should not be equated with that which the natural scientist calls "indeterminate." Contemporary physicists seem to have discovered in the sub-atomic realm a sphere in which no predictable pattern for individual particles can be discerned. Regularities in behavior of masses of such particles can be predicted with varying degrees of probability, but not the behavior of individuals. The theological conception of spontaneity, however, though it by no means excludes the sub-atomic realm, comprehends the "lawful" as well as the "unlawful" in the whole of nature. In relation to the creative rule of God and its powerful establishing, every natural entity is open to new developments, the stone as well as the photon, the planet as well as the electron.

Continuity

The natural world also has a thoroughgoing continuity corresponding to its determination by the wise shaping of the creative rule of God. To say that nature is continuous is to say that everywhere and at all times the constituents of the natural world flow from their antecedents and move in the direction of their descendants. And although this is an analytical statement, it is not for that reason trivial. It denies that nature is a chaos. It affirms that nature does not live, move, and have its being without being shaped wisely by the creative rule of God.

It is no accident, in other words, that the sun rises every morning, that an oak tree grows from an acorn, that man emerged from an apelike creature thousands of years ago (and did not spring fully developed into the world as Athena was born from Zeus' forehead). Without commiting oneself either to a traditional (Aristotle, Aquinas) or to a contemporary (Teilhard de Chardin) conception of natural teleology, one can say from a theological perspective that natural entities are characterized by an "inner law" (Tillich) which is the created parallel to the wise shaping of nature by the creative rule of God. Nature may be fittingly likened to the turbulence of a swift river (spontaneity) which is also *channeled within a well-marked course;* that is its continuity.

As the creative rule of God which establishes and shapes nature is not opposed to itself or divided, the corresponding created moments of spontaneity and continuity are not opposed. This is not to deny that the one or the other may predominate in any given place or time. Sometimes the new in nature may indeed come to the fore; sometimes the elements of continuity may predominate. Borrowing a term from physics, used with regard to the question whether light is constituted by particles or waves, we can perhaps refer here to the *complementarity* of spontaneity and continuity. The two are balanced, in other words, and play harmoniously, each one with the other, now one now the other coming to the fore, depending on the time and the place and our own apperception of both.[4]

Congruity

A third moment of the created existence of nature is its congruity, which corresponds to its determination by the joyous valuing of God. Nature's congruity is its perfect fulfillment of its determination by his rule. The biblical writers sometimes suggest such an idea in their call to nature to praise God.

> Praise the Lord!
>
> * * *
>
> Praise him, sun and moon
>   praise him, all you shining stars!
> Praise him, you highest heavens!
>
> * * *

Let them praise the name of the Lord!
For he commanded and they were created.
And he established them for ever and ever;
he fixed their bounds which cannot be passed.
Praise the Lord from the earth,
you sea monsters and all deeps,
fire and hail, snow and frost,
stormy wind *fulfilling his command!*
Mountains and hills,
fruit trees and all cedars!
Beasts and all cattle,
creeping things and flying birds!
(Ps. 148:1, 3, 4a, 5, 6, 9f.)

Here nature is depicted as a reality established by the Creator and praising him by remaining within the bounds he has set. Accordingly, nature's congruity is its perfect fulfillment of the will of the God. It is the perfect correspondence of its spontaneity and its continuity to the establishing and shaping moments of the Divine rule.

The poetic image of nature praising God suggests an image of God joyfully receiving that praise. This makes the idea of nature's congruity a significant addition to the ideas of spontaneity and continuity. It implies that God is pleased with what he sees. Without the idea of congruity it might be asked whether the notion of a Divine rejoicing has any actual reference to nature or whether it is not purely an inner-Divine act. The idea of congruity suggests that God actually has something to see, as it were, when he looks at the creation and sees that it is good.

Nature's congruity has a twofold character. On the one hand, its congruity is its perfect correspondence to the creative rule of God so that God might rejoice *in nature itself* as an ultimate end. Nature in itself offers every assistance—one thinks here of its variety, its immensity, its infinite complexity—

to make the rejoicing of God complete, both now and in the time of the new creation. On the other hand, nature's congruity is its perfect correspondence to the creative rule so that God might rejoice in *nature as a subordinate end posited for man's sake.* Again we see that nature in itself offers every assistance—one thinks of its submissiveness before man's dominion and its provision of food and clothing for man to facilitate a fullness in God's rejoicing. In these two ways, then, in itself and as a servant for mankind, nature perfectly serves the Divine joy. This is perhaps why the Psalmist surveys heaven and earth, as they are "established" and "appointed" by God, and then proclaims, "all things are thy servants" (Ps. 119:89-91; cf. Ps. 104:4). Nature in its congruity is fit to be an object of the Divine rejoicing.

Against this background of nature's life of its own in spontaneity, continuity, and congruity before God, we can now fittingly consider the point where the two dimensions of the created realm, the natural and the human, are united. This brings us to the perimeter of the life of man.

2. The Life of Man in Nature

Since man is a moral creature, the ethical side of his relationship to nature is of paramount interest to us. We will want to consider how man is able to step back from nature in order to control, care for, and wonder at nature, how he is created to live *with* his fellow citizen. Yet how man lives with nature is actually inseparable from what man is *in* nature. So we must consider at the outset his immanence in nature. This has to do with the very fabric of human self-understanding: man is a fellow citizen of nature only insofar as he is *essentially united with nature.*

Man's life *in* nature has two aspects, his relation to his body on the one hand and to the whole world of nature on the other. My body is something special to me, even though I am quite aware that it is a constituent of the whole world of nature. Theologically, this existential sense for the specialness of the body is affirmed by the biblical idea that man alone, among all the creatures, is created in the image of God—a notion which contains an important reference to man's bodiliness. So in considering man's life in nature, we will look first at the *intensive* aspect of man's union with nature, the soul-body relationship, and secondly at the *extensive* aspect of man's union with nature, the self-world relationship.

Soul and Body, Body and Soul

Concerning man as soul and body, Karl Barth has stated, "man *is* the soul of his body."[5] It could also be added that man *is* at the same time the body of his soul. Man is a psychosomatic unity, in other words, not merely a soul using a body, as Barth sometimes seems to suggest. Barth tends to view soul and body as being set over against each other (although he also wants to say that man is not man without his bodiliness), that is, man should be seen mainly under the rubric of transcendence. Barth treats the soul's relation to the body chiefly as the relation of I to It, as the relation of the subject which stands apart from a mere object in order to manipulate it. It is both possible and necessary to say, however, that *the soul also cooperates with and follows the body,* allowing the latter to actualize its intrinsic possibilities. This is what it means to say that man *is* the body of his soul. Man's body and man's soul are original and integral constituents of his existence; the body is not a mere platform for the soul.

It is interesting that the biblical expression "the image of

God" refers to the whole man, body and soul–with the accent perhaps lying most heavily on man's corporality.[6] Luther was not without exegetical grounds when he commented that "The fact that Adam and Eve walked about naked was their greatest adornment before God and all creatures." Luther did not devaluate the body as compared with the soul, but affirmed it as an integral constituent of man's being.

This unitary conception of soul and body comes into sharper focus when we explore the problem of self-understanding. What do these fingers and these eyes and these legs have to do with my self? Are they merely instruments of it, allowing it to be efficacious in the world of space and time, or are they intrinsically constitutive of the self? One may answer that to myself, I am body-soul. I do not need to penetrate behind my body to find my true self. When another encounters my body, he is already encountering my true self. Speculation about my soul inhabiting another body at another time and place, accordingly, is nonsense.[7] I am not "me" apart from the hands and muscles, sensations and reflexes which I know are mine. I can understand therefore why bodily growth or bodily injury affects my whole personality. *I am the body of my soul* as well as the soul of my body.

But, it may be asked, if the self includes the body, does this not seriously limit the created freedom which we know the self enjoys? As a part of nature is the body not locked in an autonomous or quasi-autonomous chain of causality, stretching from the past into the present? Does the self not have its freedom precisely by virtue of being *above* the chain of natural causality? For some, it has seemed a self-evident truth that "as regards this empirical character [of man] there is no freedom" (Kant).[8] But as a theological conception this "self-evident truth" must be said to misrepresent the facts. For as we have seen, nature properly considered is not a self-sufficient enclosed machine but a flowing, turbulent river, totally dependent from moment to moment on the immediate and continuing creative rule of God. In itself, correspondingly, it has a spontaneity, an openness to new developments. Nature is not locked in a prison of perpetual sameness. This is as true of the human body as of the tree on the mountain side or the galaxy proceeding through outer space or the photon in its path. This means there is a fitting union of the spontaneity of the body happily wedded to the freedom of the soul. Even more, the spontaneity of which the human body is capable is a *particular* spontaneity, insofar as it is united with the soul. Bodily spontaneity in a fully self-conscious person is taken up into the freedom of the soul, or it can be at times. As Reinhold Niebuhr has expressed it, "the freedom of man consists not only, as it were, of the windows of the mind which look out from his second story; but also of vents on every level which allow every natural impulse a freedom which animals do not know." [9]

This interpretation points us beyond the cult of compulsive manipulation's psychological consequences in what Keniston calls "the tyranny of the ego." In these terms we can now emphasize that *the ego should properly give way regularly to the vitalities of the body,* allowing them to come to their own expression, as well as governing them with a view to the ego's own ends. The self-conscious center of the personality, when it governs well, will know how to let the body dance. It will know how to say, "brother body."

The theological tradition of which Barth here is a prime example has not really known how to say that. It has viewed the body more or less as the platform for the soul, in modern terms, as an "It." And so it has played into the hands of the tyrannical modern ego. All this is not to deny that the ego should govern, that man is the soul of his body. It is just to emphasize a point too long neglected, that the body too has its rights, that man is the body of his soul. That is the intensive aspect of his union with nature.

Self and World

Man's union with nature also has an extensive aspect, the relation self and world, or body-soul and world, given with man's existence in the created realm. In metaphorical language, man is created to be "at home" in nature generally, just as he is created to be "at home" in his body. Trees, rivers, flowers, stars, desks, tables, buildings, bombs, rusty tin cans, and similar natural entities are constituents of man's homeland, however it may be distorted. Such entities do not belong to a foreign land, a land into which man may or may not travel as he pleases. If he is man as he is created to exist, he lives in the world of nature generally. Both of the creation accounts in Genesis make this abundantly clear, as do the biblical writers generally. In this sense the dictum connected with Feuerbach's name has more validity than many of his critics generally allow: *Man ist was er isst.* Man has his existence only insofar as he lives in the created realm of God which includes the world of nature. The fact that the self transcends its homeland should not be taken to imply that the self is not united with nature.[10]

To return to the language of self-understanding, just as one does not say "I" without referring at least implicitly to one's body as a constituent of the self, so *one does not say "I" unless one refers at least implicitly to one's union with the whole world of nature.* I am not the person I am apart from this table before me, apart from the lilies blooming outside my window, apart from the hot summer smell of city asphalt underneath the wheels of my car. I am not the person I am apart from the animals I know and have known, even those beasts of prey which make death a universal phenomenon in nature. I am not the person I am apart from the treacherousness of nature I have known and can anticipate, however uncertainly: earthquakes and famines, plagues and floods. Likewise, I am not the person I am apart from the polluted air I breathe, the polluted river which flows through the center of my town, and the defoliated forests and bulldozed and bombed villages halfway around the globe. All this, distorted as some of it is, belongs to my homeland in nature and helps to constitute my self-understanding.

As one's natural environment changes so does one's self-understanding, sometimes almost imperceptibly, sometimes radically.[11] (A change in natural environment thus corresponds to a change the body might undergo either in normal growth or in the loss of a limb or of sight; natural change affects the self-understanding.) A person who lives in a city slum will generally have an estimate of himself which differs from that of a person who lives in a rural area. A nomad will have a different self-understanding than a man who works the earth. An artisan will generally have a different self-understanding from a poet, and a machinist from a beekeeper. A person who lives in a temperate climate will differ from one in the tropics with respect to self-understanding, and a person living in the Arctic will differ from both of them.[12]

It was not naive or accidental, then, for the Old Testament writers to conceive of the soul, the *nephesh,* as penetrating into a person's property, into his domestic animals, and into his land in general. Although that conception may have involved a kind of pan-psychic world-view, it was not without theological underpinnings in the belief that man is created *in* the world of nature. Hence when one says "I" one includes the natural world as a matter of course.[13] To put this sharply,

Noah would have sacrificed something of his own self had he not taken the animals with him on the ark. One can recall here, too, Luther's explanation of the First Article of the Apostles Creed: "I believe that God has created me *together with all creatures.*" There is no need to deny here what theologians like Barth and Brunner affirm so often and with such conviction: that man says "I" only in relation to a Thou. But such a conception of a person's self-understanding is unduly limited. For it is just as true that a man can say "I" only in relation to the whole world of nature.

3. The Life of Man Above-and-With Nature

The life of man, inseparably united with nature, is not identical with nature. Man has his own dimension of existence within the created realm of God. This is to say that man is *above* nature, that he transcends it, both in the intensive soul-body aspect of his union with nature and in the extensive self-world aspect.

Man's life above nature has its ultimate foundation in the fact that God relates himself to man as I to Thou. God speaks his Word to man, and man hears and responds.[14] God enters into personal *communion* with man alone among all the creatures which exist in nature. Corresponding to this, man alone can enter into personal communion with his fellows and relate himself to his own kind as I to Thou. He alone can speak to another disclosing his inner side and respond in kind to the spoken self-disclosure of the other person. He alone of all natural creatures of God is conscious of himself as a self, transcending the immediacy of his present, remembering his past, anticipating his future.[15]

Whereas nature is merely spontaneous, man is free. Man is

self-consciously open to new possibilities which he may actualize when the time is ripe for him to transcend his past. Whereas nature is merely continuous, man is self-consciously able to order his life. He is able to preserve structures from his past when he wills to do so. Whereas nature is merely congruous, man worships. He can praise God with heart and soul and mind. He gives God glory with self-conscious decision, understanding, and feeling. This he does, too, in the context of a community of persons like himself, the "I" joining with other Thou's in one unified act of worship. The expression which summarizes all this is that man alone is created according to the *image of God.* While we cannot consider fully the many ramifications of this statement, we may at least take it to mean that man exhibits in his life a personal existence which corresponds to the personal existence of God.[16]

At the same time man's transcendence of nature is a concomitant transcendence. He is created not to turn away from but to engage himself consciously with nature. "Above" thus implies "with." The activity of man is to correspond to the creative rule of God. He is created to imitate in a creaturely mode God's activity with respect to nature.[17] This is an aspect of man's being created according to the image of God. As God powerfully establishes nature, man is created to be nature's overlord. As God wisely shapes nature, man is created to be her caretaker. As God joyously values nature, man is created to be her wondering onlooker. And, corresponding to God's history with nature, man is created to relate himself to nature dynamically and responsively, not statically and indifferently.

Man as Overlord

Man is established by God with the prerogative to exercise dominion over nature, as the Genesis narrative suggests. Man has been given freedom to manipulate nature, that is, to relate himself to nature in an I-It relation.

As man is soul and body, he can be said to exercise an inner and an outer dominion. By employing his spirituality he can probe into the hidden workings of nature. This is his inner dominion. He can describe aspects of nature's continuity in terms of "laws." To express the same point somewhat differently, man has the authority to give natural entities their names (cf. Gen. 2:19), and in so doing to realize an order in nature which would not otherwise be evident to him. Confronted by spontaneity, on the other hand, man can revise his description (or his name-giving) to account for new modes of nature made known to him. Such investigation can serve either as an end in itself, satisfying man's curiosity, or as a means for sustaining or bettering human life. When man does use his investigation as a means for human betterment, he can do so in the confident assurance of the Divine Word that he is worth more than the world of nature, that God exercises special care over him and takes a special interest in his destiny.

Man's external dominion over nature is exercised through the body through which he can effect his intentions, perhaps very simply, as in moving a small stone from here to there, perhaps complexly, as in constructing a machine which can move mountains. Since the world is shaped as a concordant whole by the creative rule of God, moreover, man's inner and outer dominion are not restricted to any one segment of nature. He can venture into the farthest reaches of his environment with the confidence that nowhere will he encounter an aspect of nature which stands outside the sphere of his dominion.

This is not to say that man's dominion is unrestricted. On the contrary, it is restricted, first by the Divine rule and in a secondary way by nature itself. The creaturely overlord's freedom of dominion is a *relative freedom.* The King, so to speak, does not make man Mayor of the Palace and allow him to function in the King's place with unbounded authority over the domain; this is the theological premise of the ethic of exploitation and the cult of compulsive manipulation. Rather, man is an overlord who works within the role allotted to him by his Lord, while his Lord *continues* to rule. This nuance of the biblical understanding of man's dominion we cannot afford to overlook. A warning needs to be issued since in modern technological society, especially where the "Protestant Ethic" makes it easy to identify man's ability to exploit nature with the biblically based doctrine of man's God-given dominion. From a biblical perspective, we must repeat that man's I-It relation to nature is limited. The limitation applies to the inner and outer aspects. The inner dominion is limited by the Divinely created mystery of nature. This theme is best highlighted by recalling the words spoken to Job from the whirlwind:

> Where were you when I laid the foundation of the earth?
> Tell me, if you have understanding.
> * * *
> Have you entered into the springs of the sea,
> or walked in the recesses of the deep?
> * * *
> Have you comprehended the expanse of the earth?
> Declare if you know all this.
> (Job 38:4, 16, 18; cf. Is. 40:12-26)

As the heavens are higher than the earth, so are the thoughts and ways of his Creator higher than the thoughts and the ways of man himself (cf. Is. 55:8-9). In his reflective dominion over nature, in other words, man enters a realm whose richness and fullness and simplicity and complexity he can never fully understand, at least in this life. In this respect, as in others, man is *homo viator* not *homo comprehensor*. The human soul may grasp aspects of nature's continuity and spontaneity, but never the life of nature as through a transparent glass. The creaturely overlord must always come to a halt before nature's mystery.[18]

Man's external dominion is limited by the *rights* of nature. As established and shaped by God for his own sake, nature has its own integrity in his eyes. He values it as such. For this reason the Divine Word commands man to respect nature, not to exploit it or to manipulate it compulsively. A lily adorning the grass stands with me as a genuine "other," established and shaped not just for my sake. It is not there to be used indiscriminately, for within certain limits, it has its own right to existence, to life, to fulfillment. It commands my respect.

Man as Caretaker

Closely related to man's role as overlord is his function as caretaker. Along with his freedom to imitate God in exercising dominion, he is given the freedom to follow after his Sovereign's daily care for nature. We are still concerned with an I-It relation, but the accent here is no longer on the motif of manipulation for the sake of the subject, but on manipulation for the sake of the object.

Man is established in the royal garden "to till it and keep it" (cf. Gen. 2:15). This means that wherever man penetrates into the world of nature, he must cooperate with its own life, thus assuring, insofar as he is able, its continuance in its created place. Thus Israel was commanded to let the land lie fallow so that the poor *and* the wild beasts could eat (Ex. 23:11). Similarly, the weekly Sabbath was for the ox and the ass as well as for the sake of those who worked the fields (Ex. 23:12). Also, the ox was not to be muzzled when it trod grain (Dt. 25:4). Even more positively,

> If you chance to come upon a bird's nest, in any tree or upon the ground, with young ones or eggs and the mother is sitting upon the young or upon the eggs, you shall let the mother go, but the young you may take to yourself that it may go well with you, and that you may live long (Dt. 22:6f.).

One should so order one's life that the whole of nature, including *wild* nature, can flourish. This means not only to respect nature's rights but to *act to preserve and to defend* those rights.

Man's divinely validated role as caretaker is neither absolute nor isolated. He is also called to imitate God's wise caretaking within the human sphere. God will care for those sectors of nature presently and perhaps permanently beyond man's circle of experience. Thus man's responsibility is limited from above. It is also limited horizontally by other responsibilities given him by God, in particular to exercise dominion so as to preserve and better the well-being of *man.* No single natural entity–including those animals which resemble man–is so valuable that he must care for it at the expense of his own life or the life of other men.[19]

In practice, the task of discovering what is best for the being and well-being of man is no simple task. This becomes evident as soon as we recall the obvious fact that authentic human life requires *quality* as well as quantity. A full stomach and a healthy body are not the sole requirements for a truly human existence. In addition to these, man requires depth relations with God and with other people. At the same time *man also requires a congenial and a vibrant living space if he is to be fully man.* This is true with regard to all aspects of nature, the wild, the cultivated, and the fabricated. Since today, however, the need for good architecture and city planning is widely recognized, we can concentrate our attention here on the importance of wild and cultivated nature for quality of life.

Man needs to engage himself, self-consciously and sometimes unconsciously, with nature in order to discover the depths of his own psychic and somatic life, the ways in which he shares in the being and becoming of the whole of nature. In this way he can come to appreciate his own vital forces, such as his sexuality and his will-to-power, much more deeply then he would otherwise be able to do. So also the vastness and the complexity of nature can stimulate his senses and imagination, helping him to feel and dream to his full capacity. The machined world of *1984,* in contrast, works to stifle human feeling and imagination. Beyond feeling and imagination, however, he needs nature for the sake of a sense of his own individuality, particularly,[20] insofar as individuality is cultivated by solitude and quiet.

Man also needs nature, especially wild nature, to begin to sense the full majesty of the power and wisdom of God. God is not just a little bigger than our machines—an upstairs mechanic. He who sports with the galaxies and works wonders with the sub-atomic sea of energy has the power of death and of life:—"When thou takest away their breath, they die and return to dust. When thou sendest forth thy breath, they are created; and thou renewest the face of the ground" (Ps. 104:29, 30). And we men need a sense for this power in order to hope truly for the final fulfillment of our own existence and of the whole of nature. *If there is little sense now for the powerful, wise, and rejoicing presence of God in nature, then there will be little or no hope in God to transform the world in the future.* This theme we have already touched upon bears repeating here. Man needs wild nature for the sake of his relation to God, particularly for his hope in God. Otherwise his hope will be vacuous or absent.

When we approach nature with the awareness that no single natural entity is so valuable that man must care for it at the expense of his own life we ought also to be aware of how nature can and does contribute to quality in human life, to a depth of existence which a thoughtlessly utilitarian approach can easily destroy. So today in addition to our awareness of the need for good community planning, we also need to be attuned to the need for a sensitive policy with regard to cultivated and wild nature, for agrarian planning and wilderness planning.

Another facet of man's role as caretaker is his function as *creative artist:* he can enhance nature as a work of art. Man is free to imitate that beautifying moment of the creative Divine rule which shapes nature as a concordant and beautiful whole constituted by concordant and beautiful individuals. Man is free to engage himself with nature deliberately but playfully, as God does, and thereby to create an even greater symphony of beauty in the created realm of God.

This is not the place to enter into a detailed discussion of the vocation of the artist. But the notion that man is created to *further enhance* the beauty of nature—whether original, cultivated, or fabricated nature—offers the rudiments for a meaningful and substantive theology of artistic creation. It allows us to avoid two esthetic extremes, on the one hand the notion that man merely imitates nature in creating a work of art, on the other hand the idea that he creates art *de novo,* as if the material and the hands with which he is working are not intrinsically beautiful in themselves, as if the world of nature were some intractable, inhospitable system in which man is an alien intruder. These esthetic extremes are tied too closely to the obsessive American drama of Nature versus Civilization and Civilization versus Nature. With the creative rule and created realm of God in view, we can transcend that dichotomy esthetically by saying that man is created to enhance the beauty of nature.

This view of man's role as nature's caretaker leads us yet another step beyond the ethic of exploitation and the cult of compulsive manipulation. Manipulation has been relativized: As caretaker, man works with nature as an "It," but neither exploitatively nor compulsively. As caretaker man is *sensitive* —both to the intrinsic needs of nature itself and to the essential natural requirements of man himself.

Man as Wondering Onlooker

Man also lives with nature as wondering onlooker and in so doing imitates the joyous valuing of all things by the Creator-King. Like God, in other words, man treats nature as an ultimate end. He enters into an *I-Ens relation* with nature.[21]

Man's relation to nature in the role of wondering onlooker is deliberately depicted here as an I-Ens relation in order to indicate a break with a firmly established theological position. In contemporary theological discussion, Martin Buber's and Ferdinand Ebner's description of the types of man's external relations has been so rigidly held by many that the only possible relations for man are assumed to be I-Thou and I-It. Since it has seemed to most that man cannot relate himself to nature as I to Thou (Buber is an exception in this respect), it has frequently been taken for granted that the man-nature relation must *always* be an I-It relation.

The popular I-Thou, I-It conception of man's external relations is not sufficient for an adequate theological expression of the biblical view of nature. For the biblical writers envision a man-nature relation which is wondering, joyous, contemplating, as well as manipulating, using, and observing.[22]

The I-Ens relation is characterized first of all by the existence of both terms of the relation in a *presence*. Both poles of the relation have a certain fluidity, an openness to new possibilities. The Ens, in particular, is a reality not circumscribed by the detached inspection of the human eye. To employ Buber's terminology, the Ens is primarily a presence (*Gegenwart*) rather than an object (*Gegenstand*).[23] There is, in other words, an immediacy to the I-Ens relation. The objectifying mode of human consciousness does not come between man and tree, as it does come between the two in the I-It relation.[24] In this sense the I-Ens relation is not a juxtaposition of a *mere* subject over against a *mere* object. It refers to a subjective pole *and* an objective pole bound together in an intimate community.[25]

If one remembers that the I-Ens relation is intimate and fluid and present, and that its poles cannot be drawn apart without transforming them into I and It, it is possible to describe each pole of the relation in turn. The Ens is characterized first by its *givenness*. This is how the creative rule of God in its moment of joyous valuing and nature itself in its moment of congruity, are encountered in the I-Ens relation. An Ens does not fit into a utilitarian description of the world. Like a two-dimensional painting, it confronts me directly with an inclusive claim, a claim which will not allow me to pass beyond it, as it were, to set it in a larger scheme of ends and means. It is an ultimate end. It has a duration. Insofar as it remains an Ens, it stands in the middle of my path. I do not pass it by with a fleeting glance, as I do an It no matter how long I may engage myself with the It.[26] When I come to a halt and contemplate a blossoming apple tree, for example, I do not immediately think about its cells or about the food it may produce for me (as overlord). Nor do I immediately think, for example, that the tree may need pruning (caretaking). As an Ens, the blossoming apple tree stands before me in its own right, a beautiful entity posited there for its own sake. I contemplate it and am captivated by it.[27] I do not penetrate behind its sheer givenness.

Along with its givenness, the Ens also exhibits a certain *mysterious activity*. This is how the moment of God's powerful establishing and the moment of spontaneity of nature itself are encountered in the I-Ens relation. I cannot fully predict how the Ens will behave from moment to moment. Insofar as it is an Ens, its activity and passivity will not always match my expectations. It will grow, decay, develop, stand silently still, or disappear in a way which I cannot fully understand. This will remain the case even when any scientific knowledge I have is integrated into my encounter with that Ens.[28]

The Ens also has *beauty*. This is how the moment of God's wise shaping and the moment of continuity of nature in itself are encountered in the I-Ens relation. In a certain sense the idea of beauty unites the other characteristics of the Ens which we have considered to this point, its givenness and its mysterious activity. What makes an object beautiful, of course, cannot easily be defined. One might say tentatively that the Ens is beautiful, whether in a simple or a profound way—whether beautiful in the strict sense or sublime—[29] because it is an integrated whole. It displays unity and diversity in harmony with each other. Every Ens is thereby like a great symphony. The symphony's unity is one with its diversity, though the one or the other may predominate at any given moment. Also, the symphony never loses its givenness, its claim for its own unique place, or its mysterious activity, its movement which can appear so unpredictable.

John Muir suggested much the same idea in saying that

"music is one of the attributes of matter, into whatever forms it may be organized." As a case in point Muir refers to a valley of his acquaintance: "Fancy the waving, pulsing melody of the vast flower-congregations of the hollow flowing from myriad voices of tuned petal and pistil, and heaps of sculptured pollen." [30] John Calvin, who in many ways is the spiritual teacher of Muir, has expressed the same idea: "All things above and below" are "beautifully arranged" so that they may "respond to each other in the most harmonious concert." [31]

Taken together these considerations provide an outline of the characteristics of the objective pole of the I-Ens relation. At the subjective pole of the same relation the mood of *wonder* is perhaps the most important; hence the reference to man as the wondering onlooker. Wonder includes, first of all, total attention. This is part of the significance of Luther's remark: "If you really examined a kernel of grain thoroughly, you would die of wonder." [32] One does not enter into wonder if one's attention is divided, for then the Ens would become an It. Wonder includes, secondly, an openness to the Ens, a willingness to forget preconceptions of what the Ens is or should be. As Muir once reported about a walk through a grove of tillandsia-draped oaks in the Southern United States: "I gazed awestricken as one newly-arrived from another world." [33] That is to say, to enter into wonder one must be predisposed to encounter the unexpected. One must put away the guide-book and look at the scenery with one's own eyes. Wonder also includes, thirdly, the willingness to become small and lowly, to humble oneself —especially before otherwise insignificant objects, the blade of grass, the piece of broken glass at the side of the road, the ant making its way across the picnic cloth. One must know how to allot the Ens a space of its own. One must not automatically pass it by or manipulate it or kill it.[34]

Wonder is closely related to two other moods, *repulsion* on the one hand, *delight* on the other.[35] The first is the mood appropriate for an Ens which comes from what was earlier referred to as the "dark side" of the world and what some American writers refer to as the Wilderness. The Dark Side of the world is symbolized best perhaps by Melville's Moby Dick. The white whale comes from the ocean, the ocean "which is the dark side of this earth, and which is two thirds of this earth." On gazing at the whale one feels "the Deity and the dread powers more forcibly than in beholding any other object in living nature." With the whale and the ocean in mind, one can say metaphorically with Melville: "Though in many of its aspects this visible world seems formed in love, the invisible spheres were formed in fright." [36]

If wonder is sometimes and to varying degrees complemented by repulsion, at other times and also to varying degrees it is complemented by delight. Here the music changes from Mahler to Mozart. One sees the earth not so much as two-thirds covered by dark ocean, but as framed, in Calvin's words, as a "magnificent theater." One senses that "God has stretched out his hand to us to give us the splendor of the sun and moon to enjoy." Hence Calvin instructs: "Let us not be ashamed to take pious delight in the works of God open and manifest in this most beautiful theater." [37] John Muir, following Calvin's admonition, wrote of the chain of islands off the Western Coast of Canada: "There the eye easily takes in and revels in their beauty with ever fresh delight." [38]

The mood of the subject which is perhaps most difficult to describe can be called the *sense for the presence of God*.[39] This might also be called, in Tillich's terminology, an awareness of a "dimension of depth" in the I-Ens relation. As Calvin writes of the whole creation,

For to everyone who approaches the heavenly building with a pure mind, the effect cannot but be that he is plunged into amazed adoration at the sight of the Wisdom, the Goodness, and the Power of God.

Elsewhere Calvin treats the same basic idea:

We see, indeed, the world with our eyes, we tread the earth with our feet, we touch innumerable kinds of God's works with our hands, we inhale a sweet and pleasant fragrance from herbs and flowers, we enjoy boundless benefits, but in those very things of which we attain some knowledge, there dwells such an immensity of divine power, goodness, and wisdom, as absorbs all our senses.[40]

This idea might be summarized by saying that in encountering the Ens, I am captivated by its openness to the Infinite, by an openness to a dimension which lies behind its givenness, behind its mysterious activity, behind its beauty.[41] Muir once expressed this in his own characteristic way by saying of a group of California Redwoods: "Every tree seemed religious and conscious of the presence of God." Of one Alaskan glacier he wrote: "Every feature glowed with intention, reflecting the plans of God." [42] The words of the Psalmist sum up the attitude: "The heavens are telling the glory of God: and the firmament proclaims his handiwork" (Ps. 19:1). True, God is *always* in, with, and under his whole created realm. But the sense for his presence is especially keen in the I-Ens relation, when man engages himself with nature as the wondering onlooker.

Related to this is the mood of *celebration*. This is how God's history with nature and nature's own responsiveness to that rule is apprehended in the I-Ens relation. With a view to the new creation of all things, as well as to the majesty of the present creative rule of God, I properly relate myself to nature when I celebrate the promise of God and the presence of God in nature. A proper relation thus entails praise and thanksgiving. Melanchthon states this aptly, referring to the creative activity of God as "streams of God's wisdom and goodness," and commenting that God intends to be "acknowledged and celebrated" in that flow of wisdom and goodness.[43]

With this theme of man as the wondering onlooker have we not come full circle to the very point from which we began? After all has been said, have we progressed beyond the ethic of adoration and the cult of the simple rustic life? We have, markedly, in several ways. To begin with, man's role as wondering onlooker, as depicted here, is tied to his roles as overlord and caretaker. Man can never rightfully be solely nature's wondering onlooker. Properly, the way to Walden Pond is a two-way street. The moment of wonder as a matter of course gives way to the moments of dominion and care. Delight in nature continually gives way to attending to the needs of man and nature.

Related to this, the I-Ens relation is appropriate in the context of *fabricated* nature—man-made glass, roads, machines, buildings, and so on—as well as in the context of cultivated and wild nature. This means that man can properly be nature's wondering onlooker *in the city* as well as in the wilds, where he works as well as where he takes his recreation. The theme wondering onlooker, then, by no means opposes the wilderness and the farm to the town. On the contrary, it encourages man to be a wondering onlooker within the city limits.

But above all, the ethic of adoration and the cult of the simple rustic life have been left behind, in that the primary allegiance commended here is not to nature, but to the Kingdom of God and his righteousness. One never rightfully wonders at nature, therefore, without the theme of Divine justice in the back of one's mind. This point is implicit in the observation that the way to Walden Pond is a two-way street. One may properly go out to wild nature and be there for a time. One may properly pause to contemplate the majesty of a steam-shovel penetrating the depths of the urban earth. In our day of compulsive busy-ness, indeed, many must learn anew how to be wondering onlookers. But this moment of wonder should always give way to action based on a sense of personal and social responsibility to all one's fellow creatures. That is the will of the Lord.

Looking back, then, we can see that in the created realm of God nature has a life of its own, its own citizenship. It has its own moments of spontaneity, continuity, and congruity, which correspond to its determination by the powerful establishing, wise shaping, and the joyous valuing of the creative Divine rule. Man, moreover, is essentially united with nature, both intensively (soul-body) and extensively (self-world). At the same time, he is created to transcend nature, to live above-and-with his fellow creature. He is created to engage himself with nature as overlord, as caretaker, and as wondering onlooker, and to do this sensitively and responsibly, thus imitating the creative rule of God in its moments of powerful establishing, wise shaping, and joyous valuing in the Divine history with nature. In this sense man's essential being and his Divine determination lead him to say—*brother earth.*[44] Within the created realm of God nature and civilization are fellow citizens.

This means overall that our discussion has taken us beyond the American dilemma with nature. The ethic of adoration and the cult of the simple rustic life, on the one hand, and the ethic of exploitation and the cult of compulsive manipulation, on the other hand, have been decisively left behind. And that means, specifically, that we have also passed beyond *the Church's* dilemma with nature. For the Church's dilemma, which has retarded its political involvement and disrupted its inner life, has been intricately tied to the general societal dilemma. With this American societal split overcome, the American Church should be able to be less American and more itself than ever before, as it relates itself to nature. Being more itself means–simply–attending with increased devotion to the Kingdom of God and his righteousness.

VIII. The Key to the New Horizon

Nature has its own integrity. The earth is our brother. Yet from the point of view of almost any Christian theologian, past or present, this presentation has left out the most important theological word. We have not yet said *Christ*. This obviously large empty space in the picture must now be filled in.

The question has been put most sharply in our century by Karl Barth, who organized and unfolded his twelve-volume dogmatic theology around the principle of a "christological concentration." Referring to such New Testament texts as Colossians 1:15ff., Barth virtually identified the Kingdom of God with the Kingdom of Christ. His critics have sometimes referred to this as "christomonism." It would take us too far afield, however, to deal fully with Barth's position here.[1] We will simply have to be content with the preliminary judgment that his christological concentration leads to an overly narrow interpretation of biblical thinking. We cannot deny that the New Testament is dominated by the figure of Christ and projects the origin and the final goal of the Christ-event back to the very beginning and forward to the very end of all things. But when all has been said the New Testament, like the Old, is predominantly *theocentric,* not christocentric. God and his kingly rule is the integrating core of biblical theology.

This is expressed paradigmatically in I Corinthians 15:28, where the very end of all things, the all-determining *telos* of the universal Divine drama of creation, redemption, and consummation is considered. Here the Kingdom of Christ is subordinated to the Kingdom of God:

> When all things are subject to him, then the Son himself will also be subjected to him who put all things under him, that God may be all in all.

The God and Father of our Lord Jesus Christ, not only Christ himself, is the central biblical concern, and that is why we focused on the Kingdom of God, not the Kingdom of Christ, as the conceptual framework for this study.

At the same time, it is my emphatic conviction that Christ is *the key* to the new theological horizon now before us. Christ, in the terminology of the classical theological tradition, is *the mediator*. This historical mission he performs first as the mediator who restores the disrupted present creation, and second as the mediator who represents and realizes the coming of the new creation in the midst of the present creation. Christ is the royal minister God sends to redeem creation so it may be as he intends it to be, who refashions it to be a fitting arena for the coming new creation. At the same time, Christ is the royal minister God sends to inaugurate the new creation. So the mission of Christ can be considered under two headings, which are separated only for the sake of exposition: as restoration and as foretaste.

1. The Restoration of the Present Creation

Man's relationship to nature surely is not to be found in its originally intended state in our world. Disruptive elements have entered into it through human sinfulness or estrangement. This is not the place to develop a full doctrine of sin, but the effects of man's estrangement on his relation to nature need to be identified.

The assumption here is that there has been *no cosmic fall.* The idea of such a fall was first strongly emphasized in the theology of Origen.[2] According to his schema, pre-existent rational and non-corporal substances, the *logikoi,* fell from their original eternal state (with one exception, the soul of Jesus) toward non-being. As a result, these *logikoi* were caught in a chain of material being, from the most spiritual and least material to the least spiritual and most material. For Origen, then, the very existence of such tangible entities as rocks, trees, human artifacts, and even human flesh, is constituted by a thoroughgoing estrangement from God. Their being is determined by the fall.

Origen's notion of a cosmic fall has not found a firm place in theological tradition. The view emphasized by Irenaeus has been much more in evidence. According to Irenaeus, only some creatures—man and the angels—have fallen: ". . . certain of his creatures sinned and revolted from a state of submission to God, and others, indeed the great majority, persevered, and do still persevere in subjection to him who formed them. . . ." [3] A number of theologians in the history of the Church, to be sure, have accepted the biblical notion of a Divine curse on nature. But that idea should be distinguished from the idea of a cosmic fall. "The earth indeed is innocent and would gladly produce the best products," Luther writes in a typical statement, "but [it] is prevented by the curse which was placed upon man because of sin." Calvin also refers to "innocent creatures" under the Divine curse.[4]

Luther's statement accurately reflects biblical thinking.[5] Man definitely has fallen, but the whole of nature has not. Through man's sin a Divine curse is placed upon his life in nature. This theme is especially evident in the Yahwistic creation narrative. A cursed nature is the legacy of man wherever he goes outside of the Garden. In the New Testament the same theme is in evidence, particularly in Romans 8, which does not project the idea of a cosmic fall, as is sometimes assumed. Sin comes into the world through man (Ro. 5:12). Nature, in contrast, is subjected to "futility" by God, "not of its own will" (Ro. 8:20). This reflects Old Testament teaching, particularly the story of Adam's expulsion from the Garden and the ensuing Divine curse upon the ground.

There is a more complex problem in biblical interpretation, however, when we consider the New Testament interest in demons. Evidently the demons and most similar creatures—the thrones, dominions and elemental spirits—are fallen. Are not these demons *cosmic* powers? Does this not mean that the New Testament accepts, at least implicitly, the idea of a cosmic fall? Undeniably there are some tendencies which thrust the New Testament away from the mainstream of Old Testament thinking about the innocence of nature under the Divine curse—tendencies which move some texts in the direction of Gnosticism, with its radical notion of a fallen cosmos. But here it is important to recognize the fact that for the New Testament generally the demons are *supernatural* powers.[6] The demons have a certain control in the cosmos and permeate it just as they have a certain control in history and permeate history (such as the Roman state, in some contexts). But the demons are not identical with the cosmos or human history. A herd of swine can be possessed; a man can be possessed. But neither the swine nor the man *is* a demon. Furthermore, demonic possession according to the New Testament often resembles, *mutatis mutandis,* the Divine curse on the earth depicted in the Old Testament. So we may conclude that the idea of a fallen cosmos, much in the air in New Testament times, is not affirmed by either Testament.

Sin is fundamentally *spiritual,* however we may describe it in specific terms, whether as pride or idolatry or lack of trust in God or as some other state or quality of human life.[7] In lieu of a more detailed discussion of this problem, we may think of sin as compulsive self-attention—sometimes demonic self-attention—by man and by groups of men (Luther's expression is *incurvatus in se*). However sin is described, its obverse side is *a loss, or a severe restriction of, the sense—for God's presence.* Sin means that man has fallen out of a proper relationship to God. How radical this loss has been is an important question (particularly with regard to the problem of man's knowledge of God outside of the history of redemption) but not one which the theology of nature should be required to answer. It is sufficient to say that if that loss is not total it is at least thoroughgoing. The loss of God has replaced communion with God as the determinative moment of the self.

With this loss goes the loss of a right relationship to fellow human beings and to the whole of nature. It is the latter which is of immediate concern to us here. Sinful man relates himself to nature, in which he has his life and throughout which his God rules majestically, as a predominately *godless* reality. The whole of nature becomes a neutral or even an alien, threatening reality. The vibrant sense for the presence of Deity is lost, as Luther indicated: "Even this small part of the divine image we have lost, so much so that we do not even have insight into that fullness of joy and bliss which Adam derived from his contemplation of all the animal creatures." [8] Without God, nature becomes an unexciting, neutral thing-by-itself, ruled by impersonal, mindless, heartless power—fate or demons or a predetermined, self-sufficient, necessary chain of causes and effects. Whitehead has compared the classical view of fate with the modern mechanical approach to nature:

The pilgrim fathers of the scientific imagination as it exists today are the great tragedians of ancient Athens, Aeschylus, Sophocles, Euripides. Their vision of fate, remorseless and indifferent, urging a tragic incident to its inevitable issue, is the vision possessed by science. Fate in Greek tragedy becomes the order of nature in modern thought.[9]

More specifically, *those elements in nature which are intrinsically alien to us, now threaten severely and sometimes terrify us.* On occasion pain and suffering and death stand forth from their natural habitat and come at us as if they were supernatural, demonic powers.

One can say, then, that physical suffering and physical death receive their "sting" when they are encountered by *sinful* man. At one point Luther suggests that thorns, thistles, floods, fire, and other phenomena in nature treated by us as evil "did not exist before [the fall] or at least *were not harmful or troublesome.*" [10] In other words, natural pain and suffering, in their original relationship to us in the present creation *do* induce anxiety; but this is held in check by a far deeper sense of trust and joy in the power and promise of God. But without this trust and joy in God, the intrinsic anxiety comes to be the dominating mood.

A godless, threatening world of nature thereby becomes a world under a Divine curse, as far as our sensibility is concerned. Nature becomes for us a sphere rejected by God. As Calvin writes of the biblical theme of the Divine curse:

The natural order was that the frame of the universe should be the school in which we were to learn piety, and from it pass over to eternal life and perfect felicity. But after man's rebellion, our eyes—wherever they turn—encounter God's curse. This curse while it seizes and envelops innocent creatures through our fault, must overwhelm our souls with despair.[11]

We suffer not only despair, but self-inflicted physical suffering and death. Sinful man *goes out of his way* to encounter and exacerbate suffering and death in nature. He engages in war and spreads disease. He willfully ravages the world of nature, destroying its balance, and thereby meets more suffering and death (from famines and the like). What Reinhold Niebuhr has said of man's historical existence can also be said of his natural existence. Natural catastrophes, in the context of sinful human life, are signs of a Divine judgment:

The catastrophes of history by which God punishes pride, it must be observed, are the natural and inevitable consequences of men's effort to transcend their mortal and insecure existence and to establish a security to which man has no right.[12]

In the words of King Lear,

> If that the heavens do not their visible spirits
> Send quickly down to tame these vile offences,
> It will come,
> Humanity must perforce prey on itself,
> Like monsters of the deep.[13]

Sinful man, of course, has tried to devise ways to avoid the threat of his disrupted relationship to nature. One we have already mentioned is the strategy of *attacking* an alien nature. Man stands up against the dark forces which seem to cause him despair. He opposes himself vehemently to nature as the source of pain and death, much as Ahab stood up against and attacked the white whale. This goes a good way to explain the satisfaction which men continue to reap from the sport of hunting or from such devastating entrepreneurial enterprises as strip mining. Nature is viewed as an enemy to be challenged and defeated. This motive helps to give shape to the ethic of exploitation.

A contrasting strategy sinful man has devised is a certain *romanticism.* This motive helps to give shape to the ethic of adoration. Man projects on nature the despair-free world for which he longs. He flees to nature for the simple rustic life. He steadfastly ignores the threatening dark side of nature. He may even attempt to make nature his religion. In his striking essay on "Wordsworth in the Tropics," Aldous Huxley points out that the poet could only find bliss and peace in nature because he rigorously blocked out much of its reality: Wordsworth's nature was the nice, safe lake country of England.[14]

We can look at both these strategies to attack and to romanticize nature as signs of what the biblical writers sometimes refer to as "hardness of heart" (e.g. Mt. 3:5). Sinful man refuses to acknowledge the despair in his relation to nature. He tries instead to create a world of his own imagination, a shell around his consciousness to ward off despair. He is sometimes quite successful, though one can ask whether the outcome of Ahab's story in *Moby Dick* is not symbolic of the vanity of attempting to defeat nature—being swallowed up finally by the very enemy one set out to overcome. And does not the romantic's hardness of heart eventually bring him to an even deeper state of despair? One wonders how the romantic feels about nature when he discovers, say, that he himself is about to die of cancer or that a loved friend has slipped off a rock at the coast and drowned. A person can imagine the kind happy world in nature portrayed in "As You Like It":

> And this our life, exempt from public haunt,
> Finds tongues in trees, books in the running brooks,
> Sermons in stones and good in every thing.

But close to consciousness is that sobering reminder conveyed in "A Midsummer Night's Dream":

> And ere a man hath power to say 'Behold!'
> The jaws of darkness do devour it up:
> So quick bright things come to confusion.[15]

Sinful man, in other words, returns to the scene of the crime again and again. His sin lies in rejecting the challenge of historical existence, the challenge of a life identified with the Universal Divine History with all things, in favor of worldly security. It lies in rejecting responsibility before God and following the ways of Baal or Mammon, the ways of adoration or exploitation of nature. In his sinfulness, then, despairing over his distorted relation to nature—which has now become for him a world without God, a world which burdens him with meaninglessness and bruises him with suffering—man returns to reenact the very patterns which lie at the roots of his plight. He is like the alcoholic who cannot stop drinking. With inner desperation he seeks to adore nature. Continually he seeks to exploit nature, with inner desperation. Continually he acts out his estrangement. To no avail. He goes around in a circle getting nowhere. Glimpses of bright things he may have, and they may inspire him occasionally to heroic acts of virtue. But the jaws of darkness do devour it up. That is the fate of his estrangement.

The coming of the rule of Christ radically changes man's life in nature. When we think of Christ, we should not think of him only as surrounded by a people who believe in him—as Barth, for one, continually reminds us to do. We must also think of him as surrounded by the whole creation. As Luther says, "When God moves the Son into our vision he includes all creatures; for God gave him everything on earth." [16] Remembering that the disruption lies in man's relation to nature, not in nature in itself, however, we will see Christ's coming as presently affecting the man-nature relationship, *not* the whole of nature directly. This is the proper scope for a biblically oriented "cosmic christology." [17]

It would be oversimplified to say that with the coming of Christ the life of man in nature is restored to its pristine moment. But we can say that the coming of his rule works to restore the man-nature relationship to its originally intended moment for those who identify themselves with the Kingdom of Christ. His rule helps to dispel the despair with which sinful man encounters nature and the concomitant awareness of a Divine curse on nature. Christ is the one who brings *peace* to man's life in nature. His disciples received him as the One who pushes back the threatening dark forces: "And he awaked and rebuked the wind, and said to the sea, 'Peace! Be still!' And the wind ceased and there was a great calm" (Mk. 4:39).[18] The same motif is present in Colossians 1:19f.:

> For in him all the fullness of God was pleased to dwell, and through him to reconcile himself all things, whether on earth or in heaven, making peace by the blood of his cross.

This sense of peace made possible through the coming of Christ was exquisitely expressed by Milton in "On the Morning of Christ's Nativity."

But peaceful was the night
Wherein the Prince of light
His reign of peace upon the earth began:
The winds with wonder whilst
Smoothely the waters kist,
Whispering new joys to the mild ocean,
Who now had quite forgot to rave,
While birds of calm sit brooding on the charmed wave.[19]

Within this framework of peace, the original moments of man's relationship to nature can begin to take shape.

The coming of the rule of Christ, we can say, demythologizes nature. It has the effect of dispelling the rule of fate or the rule of demons or the rule of a dark, self-sufficient chain of cause and effect. The coming of the rule of Christ discloses to us the creative rule of God.[20] The despairing relationship to nature is put aside, and we can contemplate the natural works of God Our Father: "Consider the lilies of the field, how they grow; they neither toil nor spin; yet I tell you, even Solomon in all his glory was not arrayed like one of these" (Mt. 6:28-29). More particularly, the coming of the rule of Christ allows us to *wonder* truly at the works of God. As Luther writes,

We are now living in the dawn of the future life; for we are beginning to regain a knowledge of the creation, a knowledge forfeited by the fall of Adam. Now we have a correct view of the creatures, more so, I suppose, than they have in the papacy. Erasmus does not concern himself with this; it interests him little how the fetus is made and formed and developed in the womb . . . but by God's mercy we can begin to recognize His wonderful works and wonders also in the flowers when we ponder his might and goodness.

The coming of his rule also allows us to delight in the *beauties* of nature. Again, to cite Luther:

> Now if I believe in God's Son and bear in mind that he became man, all creatures will appear a hundred times more beautiful to me than before. Then I will properly appreciate the sun, the moon, the stars, trees, apples, and pears, as I reflect that he is Lord over all and the center of all things.[21]

Another way of saying this is that the coming of the rule of Christ works to reinstate the fullness of man's I-Ens relationship to nature. At the same time, it reinstates, in proper proportion, the I-It relationship. Under the rule of Christ the believer is free to relate himself to nature in a balanced way, as its overlord, caretaker, and wondering onlooker. The Christian true to the Kingdom of Christ will never attempt to attack or to lose himself in nature, or even to be indifferent to nature. On the contrary, he will daily strive to use nature with respect and for the sake of his fellows. He will daily strive to care for it, but not without regard to the needs of other men. And he will daily open his eyes and ears to wonder at nature as a symphonic constellation of Divine activity; though, again, not at the expense of his fellows.

This new relationship has a special link to the work of Christ. The restoration of man's original relationship to nature flows preeminently from the *Cross* of Christ, as the writer of Colossians suggests: ". . . through him to reconcile to himself all things, whether on earth or in heaven, making peace by the blood of his cross" (1:19). This peace, as we have seen, provides the new framework in which a restored relationship to nature can develop. As the believer more and more identifies himself with the death of Christ, into which he was baptized, he more and more "dies" to his sinful relationship to nature and enters into that authentically human relationship in which he is created.

2. The Foretaste of the New Creation

But the coming of the rule of Christ means more than the restoration of the present creation. Christ, especially in his Resurrection, is the "first fruits" or the "foretaste" of the new creation (cf. I Cor. 15:23). In Christ the believer finds both the release from despair *and* the vibrant promise of a totally transformed existence. As Luther writes, "We are waiting for that life for which Adam also should have waited." [22] For Irenaeus, who conceived of Christ's work not only as a restoration but also as a completion or perfection of creation, the coming of Christ meant that creation was being made into something richer than it had ever been before.[23]

As the harbinger of the new creation, the coming of the rule of Christ is the beginning of the end of the dark side of nature, the end of physical pain, suffering and death. He makes all things new (cf. Rev. 21:5). The rule of Christ accomplishes this through both the person of Christ and the promise of Christ for the whole world. That is to say, the new creation is *not yet* with regard to the whole of nature and history (cf. I. Cor. 15:23). This apparently is at least part of what Paul means when he says:

> We know that the whole creation has been groaning in travail together until now; and not only the creation, but we ourselves, who have the first fruits of the Spirit, groan inwardly as we wait for adoption as sons, the redemption of our bodies (Ro. 8:22f.).

But the new creation is *now* with regard to the resurrected Christ himself, who rules throughout the whole creation.[24]

The Final Future of the whole universe is now present in the person of Christ and his rule. He is in the midst of the world as the proleptic reality and the vital promise of the final fulfillment of all things.

The rule of Christ is *fittingly* in the world in this way. The presence of the resurrected Christ is like the creative rule of God generally. If nature were a closed, self-sufficient system or machine, of course, then it is indeed difficult to see how the rule of the resurrected Christ is fittingly situated in the midst of our world. But if nature is totally dependent from moment to moment on the effectual rule of God, a perfectly supple reality which cordially responds to his slightest touch, then the resurrection of Christ can be understood not as a strange interruption of the course of nature, but as a *continuous extension* of the Divine creativity, albeit an extension which is "much more" than any other creative act of God. For the resurrection is not unlike any natural occurrence. The resurrection is *the* wondrous event, but only in the context of a world which itself is full of wondrous events.[25]

"The Resurrection of Christ does not violate nature, but only death," says Richard R. Niebuhr.[26] From this perspective, we can see the truth of the dictum, *natura spirat resurrectionem.* The coming-to-being of life in the midst of death throughout the present creation, as in the case of the death of one animal to give food for the life of another, is vindicated finally by the new creation, begun in the Resurrection of Christ from death. This does not alter the fact that in the present creation life and death exist side by side, and one after another, in such a way that—apart from the hope of the new creation—one cannot discern which is the more fundamental reality. Nature in itself is a highly ambiguous teacher. Only when the restored present creation is seen as fulfilled in and through the resurrected Christ and his rule, can one say with St. Francis, "Brother Death." For only from this standpoint, next to the living Christ, is death unambiguous. Only here is it revealed as the way to eternal life in the fulfilled Kingdom of God.[27]

The Church celebrates both the restoration of its relationship to nature and the foretaste of the new creation in its communal worship. All of the Church's worship, when it is right, is *sacramental.*[28] The crucified and risen Christ is present, in, with, and under the fullness of the church's gathered worship. Thus in the eucharistic meal believers recall and identify themselves with the death of Christ and enter into communion with the Christ living as the first fruits of the new creation.[29] In this context, the material elements, bread and wine, and the material actions, the breaking of the bread and its distribution, themselves partake of the reality of the new creation. Within the life of the Church, in other words, our eyes and our hearts are not only opened and directed to an authentically human relationship to nature in this present world, but to the first fruits of the coming Omega-world. In communion with the risen Christ we gain a sense of what nature will be like on the Final Day.

We should not overlook in this context the waters of baptism, the bodily movements and actions involved in preaching and hearing the Word, and the bodily proximity within the gathered worshipping community (cf. the "kiss of peace").[30] The natural aspect of the Church of Christ is not a closed door, as it were, which must somehow be broken down or by-passed in order to enter into the presence of the living God and his Christ. The natural dimension of the Church's life is an open door for those who believe, through which they may enter, immediately and intimately, into the presence of Christ.

The presence of the new creation in the life of the Church, like the presence of the resurrected Christ in the world generally, is not a foreign intrusion into nature as it is created: it is a wondrous event fittingly situated in a world pregnant with wonders. Although it transcends the natural aspect of the Church as the Resurrection itself transcends the world of nature, the point to be emphasized is that the presence of Christ in the Church is not an alien intrusion into a self-enclosed world, but fundamentally an *extension* of the paternal rule of God himself.

The emphasis has been anthropocentric in this presentation, since the source of the disrupted man-nature relation is located within *man* and since the fruits of the new creation are tasted now in the Church by *man* in communion with Christ.[31] The balance between the anthropological and the cosmological can be quickly restored, however, by recalling that the final coming of the Kingdom of God, the new creation of all things, will be a day for the whole of nature. This is expressed ably by Luther in a comment concerning the healing work of Christ. Christ first heals through the forgiveness of sins, Luther remarks, and this is mediated through the Gospel and the sacraments. But in and through Christ much more will be done on the Last Day:

> Then the hurt will be bound up completely and the wounds healed altogether and we shall be healthy, sound, and pure in body and soul. Then there will also be a new heaven and a new earth, the light of the moon will be as the light of the sun, and the light of the sun will be sevenfold, that is, immeasurably brighter than it is now. . . . That will be a broad and beautiful heaven and a joyful earth, much more beautiful and joyful than Paradise was.[32]

We must conclude by reminding ourselves again that *omnia exeunt in mysterium*. Presently the life of the Church is "hid with Christ in God" (Col. 3:4). Now the Church sees neither the fullness of the present creation nor of the new. Rather, we have faith and we have hope. We see through a glass darkly. And on that clouded vision the proclamation of the integrity of nature finally depends. When all has been said, it is a venture of faith and of hope to say "brother earth."

IX. Toward an Ethic of Responsibility

"So every sound tree bears good fruit," Jesus says in the Sermon on the Mount, "but the bad tree bears evil fruit" (Mt. 7:17). The test of any theology is its ethical pay-off. The most beautiful and coherent theology, without good works, is all for naught. This is particularly true for the theology of nature, which covers terrain that in the past has consistently produced such bad fruits.

As we have seen, the nineteenth-century ethic of adoration and its twentieth-century counterpart, the cult of the simple rustic life, have prompted countless Americans to turn away from the social challenges of the city of man. An idolatrous relationship to nature has occasioned what is always close on the heels of idolatry, an easy acceptance of an unjust status quo. If God is in the wilds and not with men in the city, he must not really care much about the problems of the city.

The nineteenth century ethic of exploitation and its twentieth century counterpart, the cult of compulsive manipulation, have prompted countless Americans to disregard the rights of nature, to deal with the earth capriciously and avariciously. If God has tied his providence to the "progress" of mankind and given man dominion over nature and a manifest destiny, nature becomes merely the raw material for the glorification of man.

This is not to suggest that the ethic of adoration and the ethic of exploitation have always had rotten roots and rotten fruits. There is something profoundly attractive in both Thoreau's sense for the wilderness and Emerson's celebration of the railroad. Mankind needs the wilderness and it needs technological progress. But those attractive elements, with relentless if not demonic cadence, have been suppressed by the negative. The proof is in the pudding. And a messy porridge this society is today. Notwithstanding heroic efforts by a few, our cities continue to decay. Notwithstanding heroic efforts by an even smaller number, our natural habitat continues to be ravaged, defaced, and polluted. The President's 1971 budget proposals symbolize the nation's plight. For housing he proposed $1.4 billion, while space exploration–which allows us to soar physically or mentally away from urban rot–is to be allocated $3.4 billion. For air pollution control he proposed $106 million, while the Super Sonic Transport–a plane which will allow us to fly beyond the speed of sound around the world for reasons nobody has quite explained, smashing the eardrums of the planet–is to be allocated $275 million. All this is coupled with a pious cry for paying reparations to nature!

Meanwhile, *time* is of the essence. The world–we must keep saying it again and again to ourselves–is facing a monstrous ecological crisis. The planetary future of mankind is truly in doubt. Unless we act now, certain trends in evidence today will become iron laws of our tomorrow. These trends will become our chains, weighing us down, binding us to a fate truly worse than death–human life without quality, without vitality, without humanity–and eventually carrying and dragging us to the loud or whimpering death of our world as we now know it.

For the next few decades, however, we *will* have a chance.

During this time the population explosion, the exhaustion of natural resources, and massive pollution can be handled—with a massive investment of imagination, technology, and political power. The frightful trends of the ecological crisis are still reversible. If we act in time!

Much the same thing can be said of the intramural ecological crisis which the Church is also facing. The Church's involvement in society definitely has been retarded by its acceptance of the cult of the simple rustic life. Its inner life,—its faith, love, hope, and biblical understanding—has also been seriously debilitated by an overall adherence to the cult of compulsive manipulation.

Yet there still seems to be some time left for the Church to repent, to shake itself loose of all vestiges of the ethic of adoration and the ethic of exploitation. How much time is very difficult to say. One cannot measure the spiritual decay of the Church by the same empirical criteria one uses to measure the pollution of the earth. There are those who argue with some force, however, that the future of the Church in America is very much in doubt, given its continuing political retardation and continuing inner malaise. Be that as it may, the Church would certainly be foolhardy to assume that it can take its time dealing with its intramural ecological crisis. Time is of the essence for the Church as well as for society as a whole.

The present situation in our society and in our Church calls urgently for an *ethic of responsibility* built on a deeper understanding of our relationship to nature. The ethic of adoration and the ethic of exploitation and their twentieth-century cultic heirs are no longer acceptable alternatives. What, then, will this ethic of responsibility be like? How will it differ from the other two? We have been considering some of these questions at various points along the way. It now remains to underline a few points in conclusion.

The ethic of responsibility will be predicated on an acceptance of what was earlier referred to as the challenge of historical existence. The claims of the socially reactionary gods of nature, the Baalim, will be rejected. The cosmocentrism of a Thoreau will be put aside. Likewise, the claims of the hyper-civilized gods, the pantheon of Mammon, "money," "success," "an ever increasing Gross National Product," and their ilk, will be rejected. Anthropocentrism, after the fashion of a Henry Ford, will be set aside. Baal and Mammon will be overthrown in the name of the God of Abraham, Isaac, and Jacob, the Lord and Father of Jesus the Messiah. Theocentrism, in the tradition of an Isaiah or a Jesus, will be the ultimate framework for defining human existence. And this theocentrism will have a concrete shape, allegiance to *the universal history of God:* the Divine rule with all his creatures, man and the whole of nature, from the very beginning through the present to the final consummation. When I identify myself existentially with that universal history, then I am responding to the challenge of historical existence.

The ethic of responsibility will be predicated on a vision of the Kingdom of God and his righteousness as the ultimate framework for judging and inspiring moral action. No longer will either nature or civilization provide the ultimate norms for human life, either explicitly or implicitly, for both will be subordinated to the Kingdom of God. Baal and Mammon will be demythologized, their former dominions subordinated to the lordship of Yahweh and Christ. Nature and civilization will be fellow citizens of the Kingdom. The Kingdom of God, as creative rule and created realm, binds the life of man to the life of nature and gives him responsibility for and to nature, as well as for and to his fellow human creatures. It gives man both the freedom and the motive to call the earth his brother.

In light of the contemporary situation it is evident that man has fulfilled neither his responsibility to the earth nor to his fellow human creatures. The righteous claims of the Kingdom of God clearly have not been acknowledged. Instead, man has devoted his energies to establishing his own kingdom, either away from the city with Baal, or in it with Mammon. The ethic of adoration and the ethic of exploitation are visible signs of man's refusal to live in the Kingdom of God.

The Kingdom of Christ calls man back to his intended role in the Kingdom of God. The Kingdom of Christ is a power given graciously to restore man to his rightful responsibility, a gift of new freedom to be authentically human. That is the faith of the Church, however dimly individual Christians may have perceived it, however falteringly the Church as a whole may have followed it.

The ethical maxim for the Church, therefore, is "be what you are." Liberated from the destructive sinful elements permeating the created realm of God, freed from both Baal and Mammon, living as a subject of the Kingdom of Christ, *I can be who I am.* It is my Christian freedom that I can be the creature God creates me to be. And in view of those destructive elements which still permeate the created realm, I will be that creature *zealously.* Christ graciously gave himself for us "to redeem us from all iniquity and to purify for himself a people of his own who are *zealous* for good deeds" (Titus 2:14). Given the sinful distortions of the good creation, and "awaiting our blessed hope" (Titus 2:13), members of the Church will as a matter of course go the extra mile (Mt. 5:41). To be good in a world where good is compromised requires a passionate will to overcome evil as well as a disposition to do what is good. It is not enough for the Christian community merely to *be* authentically human, as it is free to be. The Church is also called to go out of its way in order to dramatize authentic humanity:

You are the light of the world. A city set on a hill cannot be hid. Nor do men light a lamp and put it under a bushel, but on a stand, and it gives light to all in the house. Let your light so shine before men that they may see your good works and give glory to your Father who is in heaven (Mt. 5:15).

The Church must be a living model, a paradigmatic instance, of the undistorted rule and realm of the Kingdom of God on this earth. This does not mean that every member will behave the same way in every situation. On the contrary, each will have different gifts and correspondingly different tasks. Yet each will use his own gifts passionately, never flagging in zeal, aglow with the Spirit, serving the Lord (Ro. 12:3-11).

The general Christian maxim to be who you are, a responsible citizen of the Kingdom of God, and to use your own gifts with zeal, has three concrete forms with respect to the Church's relationship to nature. As we have seen, man is created to play a threefold role, as overlord, as caretaker, and as wondering onlooker. What shape should that threefold role assume today?

The traditional theme of man as *overlord* must be reaffirmed today, notwithstanding the many evil fruits which have grown from it, especially in the modern period. To deny man's dominion is to undercut his divinely bestowed freedom. And that, in turn, is to deny him the grounds to deal creatively with his environment. But as we affirm man's dominion, we must stress the two corollaries that man's lordship over the earth is relative, limited by and subject to God's kingly dominion, and, that man's dominion is not for dominion's sake, but for the sake of the well-being of all his fellows, particularly the poor.

If a hungry family asks me for fish, and I am able to respond, I will catch some fish and give them food. But if an entrepreneur asks me to help him or to permit him to build a chemical plant that will pollute a lake containing fish, I will think long and hard before I comply with that request. If no justifiable human need is to be served by the plant, then *the Divinely bestowed rights of the fish* take precedence over the Divinely bestowed dominion of the man.

But more than a negative calculus of man's dominion is required in our time. Man's role as overlord today must also be restorative. Dominion properly understood is for the sake of the well-being of mankind, particularly of the poor and the oppressed. In our time, when man has so treated the earth that its own rejuvenating forces are being poisoned, and taken goods from nature to such a degree that the day is coming when there will be no more goods left to take, man's God-given dominion must take the form of curtailment and renewal. All the wisdom, technological know-how, and political power that men of good will can muster must be directed toward the reversal of the population explosion, the abatement of pollution, and the termination of the rape of the world's resources. Along with this, food and shelter must be given *en masse* to the hungry and the dispossessed.

If this corrective use of man's dominion is to be anything more than pious talk, moreover, we must be prepared to make thoroughgoing changes in our social mores and social structures. The cult of compulsive manipulation–the pattern of dominion for dominion's sake, the habit of production for production's sake–must be undercut at its social roots. The Gross National Product must be demythologized! We can appreciate this need simply by noting how greatly dependent America's gigantic GNP is on resources imported from underdeveloped countries, whose peoples need them much more than we do. An ever increasing rate of productivity can no longer be the criterion of national health; if anything, it must henceforth be the criterion of national disease.

We must use our God-given dominion to reverse the results

of centuries of dominion for its own sake which still flow from our present day economic system. It will be well to remember as we plan and undertake the momentous social changes we need that our primary allegiance is to the Kingdom of God and his righteousness, not to any particular economic system. Let us have no illusions at this point; our system of corporate capitalism may have to go (so too may the Soviet Union's system of communism). For the sake of the people of the earth, and for the sake of the earth itself, the Church may well have to pursue a radically responsible role in the Kingdom of God, lest we find before too long that we have no world left over which to exercise our dominion, that we are overlords with no domain.

What is true for the Church as a body is also true for every individual member of the Church. The individual too must learn anew how to seek first the Kingdom of God and his righteousness, to exercise dominion responsibly. Particularly those who are affluent today must come to understand that the resources of our brother the earth, like the resources of any creature, are finite; that excessive consumption with little or no effective recycling cannot go on forever; and that Americans consume a scandalously inordinate amount of the earth's resources.[1] So the question of *new life-styles,* raised in many quarters today, is a question of real urgency.

Every citizen of the Kingdom must be able to meet anew—in a germane contemporary mode—the test Jesus put to the rich young ruler, who had followed all the commandments but who still remained "very rich" (Luke 18:18ff.). Do we need all those power-hungry air conditioners for example? Do we need that air-poisoning second car? What about the first car? Furthermore, can we blithely and literalistically follow the Genesis injunction to "multiply and fill the earth"? What about the size of our families?[2] And, never to be forgotten, how can we responsibly employ the resources we save by our ecological self-discipline?

These questions and many more like them must be raised today, above all by those whose identity it is to be a light to the world. To help us set a righteous ecological example, we may well find new relevance in the somewhat neglected early works of the German theologian and martyr, Dietrich Bonhoeffer, especially his rigorous study *The Cost of Discipleship*. Likewise, we will surely want to remember St. Francis today, not only as the one who called all his fellow creatures brother and sister, but also as the one who, following Jesus, shaped his life by poverty. Indeed, can the citizen of the Kingdom legitimately say "Brother Earth" today without also saying with St. Francis—each one in his or her own context [3]—"Lady Poverty"? That is a question every affluent disciple of Jesus must ponder today as he seeks to work out his personal pattern of responsible dominion over the earth.

William James once spoke about the need for society to identify a moral alternative to war. The same might be said today about Western man's traditional propensity to exploit nature. That aggressive habit has undoubtedly established a meaningful milieu for the lives of many. To this very day the challenge of developing a new process for the exploitation of nature or the challenge of making a business continually increase its rate of production is of profound existential attraction for many. What are we to give people in place of the cult of compulsive manipulation? What is a moral alternative to the Gross National Product? Giving men the challenge of correcting the error of the past and renewing the earth will perhaps be one thing. But a theology of the Kingdom of God can offer them more.

As a responsible subject of the Kingdom of God man is also to play the role of *caretaker*. This is the challenge, first of all, to take care of nature for nature's sake, to work and plan so that nature may just *be*. At this point the natural sciences, particularly the young science of ecology, can be of decisive ethical help by describing for us nature's pattern of being, particularly the system of relationships (eco-systems) obtaining throughout nature. As one ecologist has written,

> Modern studies on animal and plant populations have clearly demonstrated . . . that nature is not a chaos of warring factions but a complex and intricate system of balances in which all living things share and to which they all contribute. The consequence of this fact is that the richer a natural community is in forms and species, the greater its inherent ability to absorb shocks from the outside. In other words, the greater the variety in a biological population, the greater its chance to survive and prosper.[4]

The responsible citizen of the Kingdom of God will work to defend the right of nature to be in its own balanced way. Indeed, he will enhance that balance wherever he can.

But man as caretaker is also challenged to care for nature for the sake of his fellow man. The obvious form of this caretaking is plowing the fields and building homes, providing the food and the shelter that men need to survive. In our day of exploding population and diminishing resources, that has become a momentous task. The so-called "hard revolution," the revolution of quantity, has yet to touch two-thirds of the world. Hunger, disease, and inadequate housing and clothing still characterize the situation of much of the world today, including suprisingly large pockets of poverty-stricken people in America. We must geometrically increase our efforts to feed, clothe, house and teach the masses on our planet. To do that, in turn, we must skillfully and sensitively and passionately care for our natural environment of life-resources.

Man is called to be a caretaker not only with respect to

the *quantity* of things he needs to survive, but also with respect to the *quality* he needs in order to enjoy a fully human life. In addition to the hard revolution, then, we must have a "soft-revolution" today. For man requires a congenial and a vibrant living space if he is to be fully human. Hence sensitive city planning is absolutely essential to human life, as is creative planning for cultivated nature. In particular some men and women can play a decisive role as creative artists. We human creatures need bread, but we also need beauty.

You say the Son of Man must live with us in sticky, stamped down
cities

* * *

That's what you say.
And the Lord is indeed the Son of Man.
Love is labor. But must not love also be exquisite labor?
Must not the diamond point of sympathetic spirit still be held, if in
reserve?
For the city once loved must still be loved.
And the spirit once healed must still be taught to sing.

These are excerpts from a poem written by a college student much dedicated to social action.[5] It tells a story too often neglected today. Man's caretaker role calls at least a few to be creative artists, visionaries who will continually be striving to enhance the beauty of the created realm of God. And the rest of us must redouble our political support for their endeavors—pushing for civic buildings, for example, like Boston's new city hall, and fighting against the construction of depersonalizing and ugly urban complexes that are all too common in our day.

Regarding the wilderness, we face a very special problem. Recently a new type of art has arisen, which has massive proportions. The artist ventures to drape cliffs with canvas, for example, to achieve a work of art. The impulse here is basically good, although the way of executing it may well prove to be merely a fad. Today we need to develop an entirely new art-form on a vast scale, which will differ from any gigantic draping of nature. We might call this wilderness art, the art of caring for our sublime wild areas with such sensitivity that their intrinsic beauty and grandeur will not only be preserved, but enhanced. This art form apparently has yet to be defined to any satisfactory degree, and we can now only vaguely conceive the shape it might finally take. But define it and develop it we must, for we need wilderness for our humanity's sake. And, in a time when these areas are daily falling to human expansion, we need to be able to find the most intense kind of "wilderness experience" in those relatively few areas we will finally be able to preserve. They must be set aside and enhanced, lest we lose touch with our own elemental roots in nature and so lose touch with our very humanity.

The third role of the responsible citizen of the Kingdom of God will play is in many ways the most attractive yet the least understood authentic human relation to nature. This is the Divine call to man to be nature's *wondering onlooker*. When man plays this role nature is for him no longer an It but an Ens. It is present to us. It has a certain givenness and mysterious activity. Above all, it has beauty. We therefore properly respond to nature with wonder, with a sense for the presence of God, and hence with celebration. All this must be set in the larger context of the universal rule and realm of God. This means that the I-Ens experience is not isolated from the fabric of human life, not an escape from social responsibility, but a moral alternative to the traditional ethic of adoration and the contemporary cult of the simple rustic life.

I walked out into the woods and I stood by a huge New

England white pine, and I was captivated by its beauty. I approached Manhattan on the Staten Island Ferry, and stood there on the deck, awestruck at the majestic skyline of the city. I walked into a Church where people were celebrating the festival of Easter, this year in conjunction with the nationwide observance of "Earth Day," and I was moved to praise the Lord in a loud voice, and to dance with my sisters and brothers in Christ for the sake of the renewal of the whole world. We glorified the Lord–for his Kingdom and his righteousness.

The ethic of responsibility thus has an intricate balance, not unlike the balance of nature itself. The overall matrix of the Kingdom of God and his righteousness allows us, if we will, to have dominion without exploitation and to drink deeply in nature without being drugged into social indifference. In the Kingdom of God nature can be both It and Ens, while the just claims of men for sustenance, conviviality, and beauty are always taken into account. In the name of Jesus, seeking first the Kingdom of God and his righteousness, we can have the best of both worlds. We can be committed both to nature and to progress. We can be instructed both by Thoreau and by Marx. The ethic of responsibility allows us to appropriate the best of the ethic of adoration and the best of the ethic of exploitation while leaving behind the worst of each one.

And more. The ethic of responsibility is gratifying and satisfying and inspiring. It prompts us not only to love our fellow men, but to *delight* in self-giving for the sake of God's Kingdom. It prompts us not only to love all our fellow creatures in nature, but to *rejoice* in our life with them. The ethic of responsibility brings ecological good fruits that are a joy to taste and to savor. It teaches us not only to say, but also to sing, "brother earth."

Appendix

Biblical Thinking and the Idea of a Fallen Cosmos

The notion that physical-vital reality is fallen, that nature is somehow intrinsically corrupt, comes into Western thinking from extra-biblical sources, especially the mythological-philosophical speculation of the platonic tradition (taken up by Origen) and the mythology of Persian dualism. Admittedly, there are themes in the Bible which seem to suggest the notion of a fallen cosmos. In the Old Testament we meet the idea of a Divine curse on the ground, for example, and in the New Testament the motif of the groaning of the whole creation as it awaits redemption. But closer scrutiny shows that the concept of a fallen cosmos is not presupposed in these instances. *Biblical thinking about the fall generally is anthropological, not cosmological.*

For the biblical writers, as a general rule, the well-being of nature before God is dependent on the well-being of man before God. The judgment resting on man for his sin spills over, as it were, on to nature in view of man's solidarity with nature. But sin has its seat in man; it comes into the world through man (or man together with *super*natural angelic forces). Nature in itself has not fallen. Nature therefore is not judged by God; it is implicated in judgment because it is the world in which man has his being. It suffers innocently under the Divine curse which is poured out on sinful man. But these points require elaboration.

As we have pointed out earlier, man is viewed in the Old Testament as being intimately related to nature. Both Genesis creation accounts make this clear. This is true at all times, too, not just when the creation is in view: man exists in solidarity with nature when he is created, when he is redeemed, and when the final Day of consummation comes, the new creation. The story of Noah may perhaps be taken as typical in this regard. Noah takes the animals, clean and unclean, with him on to the ark; and, correspondingly, the Noahic Covenant is made with "all flesh" (cf. Gen. 8:1, 9:12, 13, 16, 17).

As Johannes Pederson has shown, for the Old Testament writers the soul (*nephesh*) penetrates not only the body, but all that man possesses. There is, moreover, an especially intimate connection between man and the land. The landed property of a family, in Pederson's words, "belongs to the psychic totality of the family and cannot be divided from it." The same was true generally of Israel and its land.[1] This solidarity with the land is reflected in the very being of man: he is *adam,* the soil is *adamah.* He is created from the dust of the soil (Gen. 2:7).

Another sign of man's solidarity with the land is the pollution of it in the eyes of Yahweh consequent to man's sin (Is. 24:5; Jer. 2:7; 8:7; 3:1, 3, 9; 16:18). As a subject created to obey God in personal freedom, man is confronted with the blessing or the curse of Yahweh (Dt. 30:26-28; cf. Gen. 2:15-17). If he obeys Yahweh's command(s), he receives the blessing. If he disobeys, he receives the curse. Because he is so closely related to nature, how he responds to God's command will affect not only himself but also nature. When Israel obeys, accordingly, mountains and hills are laden with prosperity (Ps. 73:2; 65:10-14) reflecting Yahweh's blessing. When, on the other hand, Israel fails to hear or obey Yahweh's voice and thereby sins, Yahweh pours out his curse (Dan. 9:11). The image of "pouring out" aptly expresses the way the curse spills over from the people of Israel onto the land and onto nature generally:

> They have transgressed the laws,
> violated the statutes,
> broken the everlasting covenant,
> Therefore a curse devours the earth,
> and its inhabitants suffer for their guilt.
> (Is. 24:5-6a)

The curse is drastic for Israel (Jer. 4:26; Hos. 4:1-3) and for all the nations (Is. 34:4a). A cursed nature is the legacy of man whenever and wherever he sins. "Cursed is the ground because of you," Yahweh says to the sinful Adam (Gen. 3:17). This curse is dramatically reactivated at the time of the flood (Gen. 8:21).

Given the presence of sin and the curse, it was easy to conceive the land as being in mourning (Hos. 4:1-3; Is. 24:4; Jer. 12:4). The vine also mourns (Is. 24:7); and the beasts groan and cry to Yahweh because the water brooks are dried up (Joel 1:18, 20). On the other hand, when Yahweh is about to judge Babylon, for example, and Israel's salvation is in sight–and with that a renewal of the blessing–the prophet says:

> Then the heavens and the earth,
> and all that is in them
> shall sing for joy over Babylon.
> (Jer. 51:48a)

In the same vein it is especially appropriate for nature to sing when Israel is redeemed:

> Sing, O heavens, for the Lord has done it;
> shout, O depths of the earth;
> break forth into singing O mountains,
> O forest, and every tree in it!
> (Is. 44:23; cf. 49:13; 52:9; 55:12)

To say that Yahweh curses the land is *not* to say that somehow the land has sinned or fallen. In the first place man alone is given the freedom to obey, man alone is created in the image of God, and therefore man alone can sin. Secondly, sinful man can be contrasted with nature (Jer. 8:7, cf. Is. 1:2). Thirdly, that the land, especially, has not fallen seems to be suggested by the idea that it vomits out its inhabitants when they have sinned (Lev. 18:24f.; 20:22).

A similar constellation of thought is evident in the New Testament. Here again man is viewed as having his life and being in nature. He stands in solidarity with nature from the beginning to the end, as is made clear in texts like Romans 11:36 and Colossians 1:15ff. which proclaim that man and nature have the same ultimate foundations. Men *and* all other things have their source in God, their present being from God, and their final end in God. In particular, man stands in solidarity with the whole creation in "groaning" (Ro. 8:22f.), in looking forward together toward the final consummation.

Yet the idea that man stands in solidarity with nature is more implicit than explicit in the New Testament when one compares it with the Old Testament. The full picture of man's relation to nature is not drawn with such clear lines as in the Old Testament. The interests of the New Testament authors are narrower in this respect, a fact which can perhaps be traced to what is sometimes called the heightened eschatological tension in which the men of the New Testament lived. Theirs was a time in which the form of the world was passing away (I Cor. 7:31b), a time just prior to the coming of the new heaven and the new earth (Rev. 21:1). It is understandable that they did not have extensive interest in their relationship to the present world of nature about to pass away.[2]

How does *sin* effect nature, according to the New Testament? Although the attitude here is somewhat removed from Old Testament conceptions, there is a basic continuity. The New Testament knows the idea that nature can be cursed (Mt. 21:19, the cursing of the fig tree) and that nature suffers tribulation when God's judgment of man approaches (Mk. 13:24f. par.; Acts 2:19f; II Peter 3:7). This idea is particularly stressed in the sixteenth chapter of the Book of Revelation with its picture of the wrath of God "poured" on the whole natural world.

The theme that nature is cursed because of man's sin, but not fallen, is paradoxically most evident and yet most obscure in the Pauline corpus. Paul's emphasis on "cosmic powers" and the like tends to cover over the idea that nature is blessed or cursed solely because of man's obedience or sin before God. Paul says, for example, that the Galatian Christians were formerly slaves to the "elemental spirits of the universe" (Gal. 4:3). But interestingly enough, he refers in the same context to the redemption by Christ of "those who were *under the law*" (v. 5)–thereby uniting the idea of being subject to cosmic powers with the idea of being under the law.[3] Shortly before that, moreover, Paul suggests that Christ "redeemed us from the curse of the law" (Gal. 3:13; cf. Ro. 5:9). So the ideas of being in bondage to the cosmic powers and of being cursed by God's law seem to be closely related. In other words, Paul seems to assume that the powers which rule with havoc in God's creation are established by God as a curse which results from man's sin (cf. Ro. 4:15). The converse idea also seems to be implied, namely, that the curse is removed from nature when man is forgiven.[4] If, further, one can differentiate the idea of the *exousia* which Paul employs in Romans 13 from the idea of the ministers of the state as such,[5] and if we can roughly identify the *exousia* with the *stoicheia* of Galations 4, then we can say that in Romans 13 we meet our theme in an explicit way, since the rulers (*archontes*) behind whom stand the *exousiai* are said to be "servants of God to execute wrath on the wrong-doing" (Ro. 13:4). In other words, the cosmic powers–here viewed as exercising influence on the historical sphere, in politics–are established by God to bring judgment on man's sin. The cosmic powers, it might be said, serve as God's effectual wrath.

This point receives further confirmation from Paul's use of the term wrath "in a curiously impersonal way." [6] Of the nineteen times he uses the word (counting Colossians and Ephesians), only twice, Romans 1:18 and Colossians 3:6, does he include the genitive "of God." By this usage Paul may mean that wrath "is some process or effect in the realm of objective facts." [7] In other words, it could be said that Paul thinks of the cosmic powers when he thinks of God's wrath and *vice versa;* hence the tendency to hypostasize wrath as something separated from God. Corresponding to this, Paul pays little or no attention to the cosmic powers as such; he is not interested in their interrelation and he applies their titles indiscriminately: "They represent altogether a cosmic metaphysical totality, in which individual distinctions are unimportant." [8] This suggests that Paul is more interested in what the cosmic powers *do* than in what they *are* in themselves (fallen angels, etc.).

For Paul, then, the cosmic powers may be taken to represent, or function as, God's curse on the whole world, on nature as well as history. We have already considered an example from the historical sphere (Ro. 13:4), so it remains to ask whether any explicit teaching of Paul can be adduced to the effect that God has specifically subjected nature to the curse of his wrath. An analysis of Romans 8:19ff. will show that there is. Paul writes:

For the creation waits with eager longing for the revealing of the sons of God; for the creation was subject to futility, not of its own will but by the will of him who subjected it in hope; because the creation itself will be set free from its bondage to decay and obtain the glorious liberty of the children of God. We know that the whole creation has been groaning in travail until now (vv. 19-22).

It seems quite clear that the proper background against which to view this passage is the Genesis account of the Fall, especially the Divine curse of the ground.[9] This is because of the close relation between Romans 5 (with its explicit relation to the Genesis account of the Fall) and Romans 8. As N. A. Dahl observes, "Chapter 8 contains a fuller development of the themes which are briefly stated in 5:1-21."[10] He who subjected it in hope," then, can only be the God who pours out his curse on the whole creation, especially nature, in reaction to Adam's sin.[11] There is, moreover, an important difference between Romans 5 and 8 showing that Paul remains faithful to the Old Testament teaching. In Romans 5 *sin* is the immediate cause of the tragedy (v. 12). In Romans 8, the immediate cause of the "futility" is *God's subjection;* and, it is said, the creation is subjected *"not of its own will."* Here, then, there is no "cosmic fall" in the sense that there is a "human fall."[12] Sin comes into the world through *man* (cf. 5:12) not through a universal fall. Nor is there any suggestion that nature is somehow a sinful reality.[13]

The terms "futility" and "decay" can easily be interpreted

as they are here translated, as descriptions of the effect of God's curse. But it would readily fit into Paul's demonistic understanding of the world and his description of cosmic powers and wrath as closely related realities they were interpreted as cosmic powers.[14] The text seems to allow for either interpretation.

In Colossians and Ephesians, we meet familiar themes, though not in such an explicit way and also with more emphasis on cosmic powers. Men generally are said to be in bondage to cosmic powers (Eph. 2:2, 6:2). Christians, in particular, are delivered from the hold of these powers by Christ (Col. 1:13f.; 2:20; Eph. 1:22). In other words, Christ brings a cosmic peace.[15] The need for such a peace implies a prior alienation of the whole creation from God, to be sure, and a prior introduction of conflict into the whole creation. However, "nothing is said here of the how or why of this alienation; it is sufficient that this is the actual state of the world, and that Christ is appointed to effect the remedy." [16]

One last question arises concerning the biblical notion of a new creation, particularly prominent in Deutero-Isaiah, Romans 8, and Revelation 21. This theme might be taken to presuppose the idea of a universal cosmic fall. But a few considerations will show that it does not. In the biblical writings the new creation theme evidently presupposes a *historicized* approach to the created order; the world is established to have a history culminating in a final transformation. "The passing of events marked in chronological time," Brevard Childs has observed, are theologically significant in forming the content of reality." [17] This is to be contrasted to the nature-oriented religions of the Ancient Near East which thought that the only significant time is the primeval pre-creation time (*Urzeit*) and which conceived of the final time of the creation (*Endzeit*) as being a return to the beginning.[18] To express the biblical presupposition metaphorically: Adam, Eve and the whole of Paradise would have had a history and would have been transformed at the end of that history even if Adam had not sinned. Paradise is not the timeless eternal now of mythological thinking; it is the created beginning of a real history whose goal is something *new,* the final re-creation. Paradise, moreover, is created as a realm of mortality; God alone is immortal.[19] Only in the new creation, when God will be all in all, will death be no more. In biblical perspective Adam's sin is set in the context of that universal supralapsarian history, from Paradise to the new heavens and the new earth.[20] Meanwhile, human sin and the Divine curse of man's life in nature notwithstanding, the history of nature remains essentially as it was created to be. This is how biblical thinking about the new creation seems to take shape. So the burden of proof would seem to rest heavily on the shoulders of the one who would maintain that the biblical new creation theme presupposes some kind of universal cosmic fall.

In sum, biblical thinking offers little evidence for the notion of a cosmic fall. The Divine judgment on man for his sin definitely affects nature, which is cursed due to its solidarity with sinful man. *The Divine curse is an anthropological theme, not a cosmological one.* Even in those portions of the New Testament where the theme of alien cosmic powers is prominent, there is no direct speculation about their origin. Rather they are viewed as agents of the Divine judgment on sinful man, agents which can possess nature as they can possess history. In the New Testament, as in the Old, sin is essentially moral and spiritual and human. Nature in itself has not fallen.

Notes

PREFACE

1. Lynn White, "The Historical Roots of our Ecological Crisis," *Science,* CLV(1967), p. 1207.

2. The word "ecology" now belongs to common parlance. It was inevitable, then, that the term "ecological theology" would be coined. But use of this term here is intended to express more than sympathy with a popular concern. It is good to be able to employ the term alongside of the more traditional sounding expression "theology of nature," since the latter might suggest merely a theology of physical-vital reality, and not also a theology of *man's* involvement in physical-vital reality. The word "ecological" highlights the fabric of interdependent relationships between man and nature. Also, the expression "theology of nature" might be taken to imply a somewhat if not altogether passive relation to nature, when the situation today requires sensitive *action* toward nature as well as a more contemplative relationship. On the other hand, the term "theology of nature" is still useful, since it is less anthropocentric than "ecological theology," and therefore it allows us to emphasize the integrity of nature as well as man's proper relationship to nature.

3. Langdon Gilkey, *Naming the Whirlwind: The Renewal of God-Language* (Indianapolis: Bobbs-Merrill, 1969).

4. Dietrich Ritschl, *Memory and Hope: An Inquiry Concerning the Presence of Christ* (New York: Macmillan, 1967), p. 87.

CHAPTER ONE

1. In addition to the justly renowned work of Perry Miller, e.g. *Nature's Nation* (Cambridge, Mass.: Belknap Press, 1967), see Leo Marx's study *The Machine in the Garden: Technology and the Pastoral Ideal in America* (New York: Oxford University Press, 1964).

2. Perhaps the most forceful exposé of America's penchant for abuse of its land is Rachel Carson's famous work, *Silent Spring* (Boston: Houghton Mifflin, 1962).

3. One impressive writer in this field is Lewis Mumford, e.g. *Technics and Civilization* (New York: Harcourt, Brace and Company, 1943).

4. Cf. Lynn White, *op. cit.* See also Richard A. Baer, Jr., "Land Misuse: A Theological Concern," *Christian Century,* LXXXIII, 41 (October 12, 1966), pp. 1239-41.

5. The major sustained treatments of nature from a theological perspective in recent years are Conrad Bonifazi's *Theology of Things: A Study of Man in His Physical Environment* (New York: Lippincott, 1967), Allan D. Galloway's *The Cosmic Christ* (London: Nisbet and Company, 1951), E. C. Rust's *Nature and Man in Biblical Thought* (London: Lutterworth Press, 1953), and the many works by Pierre Teilhard de Chardin. None of these works however, deals with the peculiarly American context of the problem. Also, all of them have specialized concerns which do not permit them to present a direct theological response to the American situation. The works by Rust and Teilhard deal with nature chiefly in the context of the discussion between religion and science. Galloway's book is concerned to fill in the historical background and to elaborate a single dogmatic theme, cosmic redemption. And Bonifazi deals mainly with issues arising from continental, philosophical phenomenology. A comprehensive ecological theology, responsive to the American situation, has yet to be written. Hopefully this study may be able to set the stage for such a work. One concrete step has already been taken, by Frederick Elder in his book *Crisis in Eden: A Religious Study of Man and His Environment* (New York: Abingdon Press, 1970), which appeared when this book was already in its final stages of preparation.

6. See my programmatic essay, "A New Theology of Nature?", *Lutheran Quarterly,* XV, 3(August 1968), pp. 304ff.

7. Ralph Waldo Emerson, *Works,* Fireside Ed. (New York: 1909), p. 11.

8. Emerson distinguishes *art* from nature: "Art is applied to the mixture of [man's] will with the same things [sc. space, air, river, leaf], as in a house, a canal, a statue, a picture." (*Ibid.*) One can accept that definition of *art* while broadening his definition of nature: calling house and statue *nature* too, insofar as they have physical and organic aspects. Fabricated nature, then, and cultivated nature, are both art *and* nature.

9. Miller, *Errand Into the Wilderness* (Cambridge, Mass.: The Belknap Press, 1956), p. 204. Miller is referring here to dominant cultural trends in the nineteenth century. To agree with him at this point is not to deny the evidence Morton and Lucia White have adduced in their study *The Intellectual versus the City: From Thomas Jefferson to Frank Lloyd Wright* (Cambridge, Mass.: Harvard University Press, 1962) regarding a post-Civil War intellectual and reformist tradition

which was very much taken by the city and its promise. But that intellectual tradition has not been an obsessive American cultural concern. Indeed, it stands out rather starkly in contrast to the dominant cultural trends both in the nineteenth and twentieth centuries in America. Likewise, Miller's generalizations do not cover the growing contemporary literature on ecology, much of which seems to be avoiding traditional romantic American anti-urbanism (see *The Subversive Science: Essays Toward an Ecology of Man,* ed. Paul Shepard, Daniel McKinley [Boston: Houghton Mifflin, 1969]). On the other hand, this young literature has yet to have a transforming affect on the national consciousness.

10. See the illuminating study by George H. Williams, *Wilderness and Paradise in Christian Thought: The Biblical Experience of the Desert in the History of Christianity and the Paradise Theme in the Theological Idea of the University* (New York: Harper and Brothers, 1962).

11. James Thompson, *The Seasons,* "Spring," 101.

12. Miller, *Nature's Nation,* pp. 207ff. Also see R. W. B. Lewis, *The American Adam: Innocence, Tragedy, and Tradition in the Nineteenth Century* (Chicago: The University of Chicago Press, 1955).

13. Henry David Thoreau, "Slavery in Massachusetts," *The Writings of Henry David Thoreau: Cape Cod and Miscellanies* (New York: Houghton Mifflin, 1906), p. 396.

14. Thoreau, *Walden* (New York: W. W. Norton Company, 1951), pp. 350, 337f., 191, 90.

15. Thoreau, *Cape Cod* (New York: Thomas Y. Crowell Company, 1961), p. 319.

16. Thoreau, "The Last Days of John Brown," *Writings,* p. 441.

17. Thoreau, "Slavery in Massachusetts," *Writings,* p. 407.

18. *Ibid.,* p. 404.

19. Thoreau, "Plea for John Brown," *Writings,* p. 433.

20. Joel Porte, *Emerson and Thoreau: Transcendentalists in Conflict* (Middletown, Conn.: Wesleyan University Press, 1965), p. 4.

21. *Ibid.,* p. 62, cf. chap. 3.

22. Miller, *Nature's Nation,* p. 152.

23. Emerson, "Nature, Addresses, and Lectures," *Works,* pp. 15-16.

24. Emerson, "Nature," in "Essays: Second Series," *Works,* p. 167.

25. Thoreau, "Life Without Pleasure," *Writings,* p. 460.

26. Thoreau, "Civil Disobedience," *op. cit.,* p. 358.

27. *Ibid.,* pp. 365, 368, 369.

28. Thoreau, "Life Without Pleasure," *op. cit.,* p. 480.

29. I am indebted to my colleague, Prof. Duncan Aswell, for helping

me to see some of the subtleties in Thoreau's thought that had otherwise not been evident to me. However, I take full responsibility for this exposition of Thoreau's work.

30. On the attitudes of the Transcendentalists generally toward slavery, see Stanley M. Elkins, *Slavery: A Problem In American Institutional and Intellectual Life* (Chicago: University of Chicago Press, 1959), chap. IV.

31. On Emerson's political concerns, see Miller, *Nature's Nation,* chap. X; and Vernon Louis Parrington, *The Romantic Revolution in America 1800-1860* (New York: Harcourt, Brace, 1927), pp. 386-399.

32. Harold M. Hildreth, "The Silent Places."

33. Roderick Nash, *Wilderness and the American Mind* (New Haven: Yale University Press, 1967), chap. VIII.

34. *Ibid.,* p. 122.

35. John Muir, *My First Summer in the Sierra,* in *The Writings of John Muir,* Sierra Ed. (Boston: Houghton Mifflin Company, 1917-18), p. 135; all the following references to Muir's work will be in this edition.

36. Muir, *1000 Mile Walk,* p. 415.

37. Muir, *Our National Parks,* p. 3.

38. Muir, *My First Summer in the Sierra,* pp. 186f.

39. Muir, *1000 Mile Walk,* p. 303.

40. Liberty Hyde Bailey, *The Country Life Movement* (New York: Macmillan, 1911), p. 15.

41. Bailey, *What is Democracy?* (New York: Macmillan, 1923), p. 36.

42. Bailey, *Outlook to Nature* (New York: Macmillan, 1905), p. 8. pp. 134, 64, 141, 62, 11. The quote from p. 64 is from a speech by a Cornell president, with whom Bailey agrees.

43. Cf. the only slightly different philosophy held by Stephen F. Hamblin, in his characteristically entitled book *Man's Spiritual Contact with Landscape* (Boston: Gorham Press, 1923). For him, "Nature is the material aspect of the Deity, as we are both material and spiritual manifestations of the Great All-One who is in essence all spirit." (p. 287)

44. Robert D. Cross, ed. *The Church and the City 1865-1910* (New York: Bobbs-Merrill, 1967); see pp. 3ff. for this material.

45. Marx, *op. cit.,* p. 191.

46. Cited by Marx, *op. cit.,* p. 202.

47. For a more detailed treatment of the mechanical view of nature, see R. G. Collingwood, *The Idea of Nature* (New York: Oxford University Press, 1960); and Alfred North Whitehead, *Science and the Modern World* (New York: New American Library, 1925).

48. Mumford, *op. cit.,* p. 25.

49. For this material, see Marx, *op. cit.,* pp. 181 *et seq.*

50. Here, too, I am dependent on Marx, *op. cit.,* pp. 192ff.

51. Miller, *Nature's Nation,* p. 205.

52. Irving Babbitt, *Rousseau and Romanticism* (Boston: Houghton Mifflin Company, 1930), p. 301.

53. e.g., Stewart Udall, *The Quiet Crisis* (New York: Holt, Rinehart and Winston, 1963), chap. 5.

CHAPTER TWO

1. White, *op. cit.,* p. 230.

2. Wendell Berry, New York *Times,* March 3, 1968.

3. Peter Michelson, "Pop Goes America," *New Republic,* CLVII, 10 (September 2, 1967), pp. 26, 28.

4. Hal Borland, *Countryman: A Summary of Belief* (Philadelphia: J. B. Lippincott, 1957), pp. 122, 69.

5. Udall, *op. cit.,* pp. 189ff.

6. Kenneth Keniston has studied this type of American youth in his book *Young Radicals: Notes of Committed Youth* (New York: Harcourt, Brace, and World, 1968).

7. Keniston, *The Uncommitted: Alienated Youth in American Society* (New York: Harcourt, Brace, and World 1960), pp. 93, 190.

8. William Cleary, *Surfing: All the Young Wave Hunters* (New York: New American Library, 1967), p. 25.

9. Keniston, *The Uncommitted,* p. 194.

10. *Ibid.,* p. 337.

11. *Ibid.,* p. 365f.

12. David M. Gates, quoted by the New York *Times,* August 11, 1968.

13. For a careful in-depth study of some of the anthropological themes which are just touched on lightly here, see Reinhold Niebuhr, *The Nature and Destiny of Man: A Christian Interpretation* (New York: Charles Scribner's Sons, 1955).

14. See Juergen Moltmann, *The Theology of Hope,* tr. James W. Leitch (New York: Harper and Row, 1967); and Wolfhart Pannenberg, *Theology and the Kingdom of God* (Philadelphia: Westminster Press, 1969).

15. See Henri Frankfort, *Kingship and the Gods: A Study of Ancient Near Eastern Religion as the Integration of Society and Nature* (Chicago: University of Chicago Press, 1948), especially pp. 337-346.

16. The motif of creating the ideal society has had a central place in the American consciousness from the beginning, as Frederick Merk has stressed in his study *Manifest Destiny and Mission in American History* (New York: Alfred A. Knopf, 1963). Merk calls this America's "mission." It began with the quest for the establishment of religious liberty;

then it came to cover a principle of government by consent. Later, at the time of Jefferson, it was protection from the federal government; under Jackson it was power for all the people. With the Civil War the ideal was extended to include emancipation. "By Woodrow Wilson's day," in Merk's words, "it meant the Fourteen Points, and by the time of the second Roosevelt, the Four Freedoms. In all these enlargements of mission the Goddess of Liberty holding aloft her light to the world seemed to Americans to be, in reality, themselves." (pp. 3f.) But the nation consistently failed to live up to its ideal, its Divine mission of liberty. Freedom for all, especially in the nineteenth century, and most of all toward the end of that century, meant in practice increased control by the few, the entrepreneurs, and increased suffering among the masses in the cities, overcrowding, squalor, disease, unemployment, child labor, and general personal and social uncertainty. The farmers, moreover, again and again found themselves at the disposal of the large monied interests.

CHAPTER THREE

1. One of the first groups to do this was the "Faith/Man/Nature Group." Its history is instructive; see my short article, "The Struggle for an Ecological Theology," *Christian Century,* LXXXVII, 9 (March 4, 1970), pp. 275ff.

2. Gibson Winter, *The Suburban Captivity of the Churches* (New York: Doubleday, 1961).

3. Harvey Cox, *The Secular City: Secularization and Urbanization in Theological Perspective* (New York: Macmillan, 1965).

4. See my article, "I-Thou, I-It, and I-Ens," *Journal of Religion,* XLVII, 3 (July 1968), pp. 260-273.

5. Karl Barth, e.g., *Church Dogmatics,* ed. G. W. Bromiky, T. F. Torrance (Edinburgh: T. and T. Clark, 1936 *et al.*), III, ii, p. 12. Hereafter cited as *CD.*

6. See, for example, Rudolph Bultmann, *Jesus Christ and Mythology* (New York: Charles Scribner's Sons, 1958).

7. Cox, *op. cit.,* p. 1.

8. A major exception here are the theologians who are strongly influenced by Whitehead, who consistently criticized the mechanical view of nature.

9. Regin Prenter, "Does the Church Need a New Reformation?" *dialog,* I, 1 (Winter 1962), p. 20.

10. John Calvin, *Institutes of the Christian Religion,* tr. F. L. Battles, ed. John T. McNeil (Philadelphia: Westminster Press, 1960), 1. 17. 8, 10, 11. Hereafter cited as *Inst.*

11. Martin Luther, *Werke* (Weimar Ausgabe), XXXI (1), 436; cited

hereafter *WA;* cited by Paul Althaus, *Die Theologie Martin Luthers* (Gütersloher Verlaghaus Gerd Mohn, 1962), p. 101.

12. e.g. *Work and Vocation: A Christian Discussion* ed. John Oliver Nelson (New York: Harper and Brothers, 1954).

13. Cf. the words of the Belgian priest, Pierre Charles, *The Prayer of All Things,* tr. James Langdale (New York: Herder and Herder, 1964), p. 29: "I fear that almost in spite of myself, my spiritual life has become, as it were, secular. I have come to consider all the things which surround me and are the thread of my existence, as mere profane realities, instead of associating them with your mind, your memory, and your presence. I try to overlook and ignore these things, in order to look for you, far away, in the world of idea. One by one, I miss all the appointments which your providence gives to me at every hour of the day during the course of my life."

14. Calvin, *Inst* 3. 25. 3.

15. Cf. Calvin on I Cor. 15:36, *Corpus Reformatorum,* LXXVII, 556, cited and tr. Heinrich Quistorp, *Calvin's Doctrine of Last Things,* tr. Harold Knight (London: Lutterworth Press, 1955), p. 132: "He [Paul] observes that so far from contradicting the course of nature it is rather that nature itself daily presents to us the pattern of the resurrection." Similarly on I Cor. 15:41, *loc. cit.,* "It is not contrary to reason to suppose that our bodies will rise again in another form: for God causes to grow out of a single grain of wheat many pretty ears and new grains quickened by vital sap."

16. Calvin, *Inst* 3. 25. 2.

17. "First Epistle of Clement to the Corinthians," in *The Ante-Nicene Fathers,* I: *Apostolic Fathers, Justin Martyr, Irenaeus* (Grand Rapids, Mich.: Eerdmans Publishing Company, 1956), chap. xxiv. Research on First Clement has shown that the generally accepted idea that this writer is merely introducing Stoicism into Christian theology by his interest in nature is very much over-simplified. Cf. W. C. van Unik, "Is I Clement Purely Stoic?", *Vigiliae Christianae,* IV (1950), pp. 181-189; and W. Eltester, "Schöpfungsoffenbarung und natürliche Theologie im Frühen Christentum" *New Testament Studies,* III (1956-57), pp. 93-114.

18. Cited by W. D. Davies, *Paul and Rabbinic Judaism: Some Rabbinic Elements in Pauline Theology,* 1st. ed. (London: S.P.C.K., 1955), p. 174, italics added.

19. The new Confession of Faith of the United Church of Christ, for example, omits "resurrection of the body" in its final article. How could a contemporary confession of faith honestly do differently?

20. Joseph Sittler, "Called to Unity," an address delivered at the

World Council of Churches, New Delhi, 1961 (Philadelphia: Muhlenberg Press, 1962).

21. George Williams, *op. cit.,* p. 137.

22. e.g. the stress on Jesus' corporal rising, underlined by the account of the empty tomb.

23. Rudolf Bultmann, "Zur Frage des Wunders," *Glauben and Verstehen* (Tübingen: Verlag J. C. C. Mohr, 1958) I, 214; my translation.

24. Bultmann, *Jesus Christ and Mythology,* p. 15; italics added.

25. Bultmann's program and his criteria for myth are more sophisticated than I can indicate here. But nature undoubtedly plays a key role as a criterion in his demythologizing.

26. Bultmann, "The New Testament and Mythology," *Kerygma and Myth,* ed. Hans Werner Bartsch, tr. Reginald H. Fuller (London: S.P.C.K., 1954), pp. 4, 5, 8, 11f.

27. Richard R. Niebuhr, *Resurrection and Historical Reason: A Study in Theological Method* (New York: Charles Scribner's Sons, 1957), p. 105.

CHAPTER FOUR

1. The only monograph presently available is E. C. Rust's aforementioned work, *Nature and Man in Biblical Thought.* The emphasis of this volume falls mainly on comparing and contrasting the biblical view of nature with the modern scientific understanding of nature; the inner coherence of the biblical view itself does not come to the fore. The best available treatment of the Old Testament view of nature is H. Wheeler Robinson's *Inspiration and Revelation in the Old Testament* (Oxford: Clarendon Press, 1946), part I. See also the unpublished paper by W. Lee Humphreys, "Pitfalls and Promises of Biblical Texts as a Basis for a Theology of Nature," prepared for the Fourth National Conference of the Faith/Man/Nature Group, Warrenton, Virginia, November 28-30, 1969.

2. Barth, *CD* III, ii, p. 19. Emil Brunner, *Revelation and Reason,* tr. Olive Wyon (Philadelphia: Westminster Press, 1946), p. 33n. Barth's and Brunner's exclusive focus on man is not just their own; they share it with a number of biblical scholars. G. W. H. Lampe stated this view succinctly in an article several years ago: "First, the Hebrew writers about creation are, in a sense, wholly anthropocentric. Man stands at the centre of the whole picture, and the rest of the animate and inanimate world is seen as a kind of backcloth for the drama of human history. What we ourselves would call 'nature' derives its significance from the activity within it of mankind and, in particular, of the chosen people of

God. In this sense, what we call the 'natural order' revolves around man as the central point and focus which gives meaning to the whole." ("The New Testament Doctrine of *Ktisis*," *Scottish Journal of Theology,* XVII, 4 [December 1964], p. 449). This anthropocentric view is so prevalent in biblical interpretation today that it is necessary to identify it as carefully as possible.

There is undoubtedly a certain anthropocentrism in the biblical writings. That is not in question here. What is in question is the *interpretative framework* for biblical theology. The anthropocentric approach before us now is faulty not because it is anthropocentric as such, but because it presupposes a speculative, essentially Hegelian framework for its interpretation.

The propriety of this judgment is evident, in a preliminary way, when we recall the shape of Barth's thought. In Barth's schema, God's election of man in Jesus Christ is the thesis, the creation of the world as such is the antithesis, and God's work of reconciliation with man in the world is the synthesis. In this framework, it will be evident, the whole natural order is a constituent of the antithesis. It is the *condition* for the final synthesis, God's reconciliation with man. It is the *stage* for the actualization of God's redemption of man.

3. Cf. Gerhard von Rad, *Genesis,* tr. John H. Marks (Philadelphia: Westminster Press, 1961), p. 60: creation means for the priestly writer that "the way is being prepared for an exalted good, actually the final, saving good." See also von Rad's article, "The Theological Problem of the Old Testament Doctrine of Creation," *The Problem of the Hexateuch,* tr. E. W. Trueman Dicken (New York: McGraw Hill, 1966), pp. 131-43.

4. S. R. Driver, *The Book of Genesis,* 2nd ed. (London: Methuen and Company, 1904), p. 5; von Rad, *Genesis,* p. 50; Hermann Gunkel, *Genesis,* 6th ed. (Göttingen: Vandenhoeck and Ruprecht, 1964), p. 105.

5. V. 24 is: "O Lord, how manifold are thy works: In wisdom hast thou made them all." Cf. Pr. 8:30, then, concerning wisdom: "I was his daily delight."

6. Cf. Job 41:5; and Ps. 135:6, "Whatever the Lord pleases he does, in heaven and on earth, in the seas and all deeps."

7. T. W. Manson, *The Teaching of Jesus: Studies in its Form and Content* (Cambridge: Cambridge University Press, 1931), p. 163.

8. Repeated Gen. 9:12, 15, 16, 17. See also Jer. 33:19, 25.

9. Robinson, *op. cit.,* p. 10. Cf. Is. 40:26; Yahweh numbers the stars and calls each one by name; also, Mt. 10:30, "even the hairs of your head are numbered."

10. Cf. Bernard Anderson, "The Earth is the Lord's: An Essay in the

Biblical Doctrine of Creation," *Interpretation,* IX, 1(January 1955), p. 14: "the doctrine of creation affirms that every creature is assigned a place in God's plan in order that it may perform its appointed role in serving and glorifying the Creator."

11. God's being pleased is a common theme of Old Testament theology, e.g.: I Sam. 12:22; II Sam. 7:29; Judg. 13:23; Ps. 5:4, 51:19; 135:6; 149:4; Job 6:9, 22:3; Pr. 16:7; Is. 43:21.

12. John Bright, *The Kingdom of God,* pp. 28, 30.

13. *Ibid.*, pp. 65f., 67.

14. Cf. Is. 24:1 and all of Is. 24; also, among others, Joel 3:14-16; Zeph. 1:2f.

15. On these passages, see Gerhard von Rad, "Basileia," *Bible Key Words,* II, tr. J. R. Coates, H. P. Kingdon (New York: Harper and Brothers, 1958), p. 7.

16. Cf. Gösta Lindeskog, *Studien zum neutestamentlichen Schöpfungsgedanken* (Uppsala Universitets Arsskrift, II, 1952), p. 55: "Reich Gottes setz also die Neuschöpfung der Welt voraus. Diese Verbindung bleibt natürlich unverändert, wen der Begriff Reich Gottes eschatologisiert wird."

17. Cf. Is. 30:23-26; 32:14-18; 35:1f.; 41:17-20.

18. John Bright, *The Kingdom of God: the Biblical Concept and Its Meaning for the Church* (New York: Abingdon-Cokesbury, 1953) pp. 167f.

19. *Ibid.,* p. 170.

20. N. A. Dahl, "The Parables of Growth," *Studia Theologica,* V, 2 (1951), pp. 132-166.

21. On this interpretation of the word *palingenesia,* see S. E. Johnson, "Matthew," *Interpreter's Bible,* on Mt. 19:28.

22. C. F. Burney, quoted with approval by M. Black, "The Pauline Doctrine of the Second Adam," *Scottish Journal of Theology, VII,* 2(June 1954), p. 170.

23. Davies, *Paul and Rabbinic Judaism,* p. 41. Cf. also Mk. 7:37; the remarks of bystanders, after Jesus heals the deaf and dumb man, are reminiscent of Gen. 1:31, LXX; nor is it without significance that Mk. 13:9 likens the chaos which is to come to the chaos which was at the beginning, thereby suggesting a parallel between the creation which followed the first chaos and a new creation which shall follow the second chaos. In this connection, also, it is interesting to note some recent suggestions for interpretation of Mk. 1:13: "And he was in the wilderness forty days, tempted by Satan; and he was with the wild beasts." It has been argued with some force that this represents the new creation motif (Erich Fascher, "Jesus und die Tiere," *Theologische Literatur Zeitung,* XC, 8 [August 1965], pp. 561-570.)

24. N. A. Dahl, in *The Background of the New Testament and Its Eschatology,* ed. W. D. Davies (Cambridge: Cambridge University Press, 1956).

25. Oscar Cullmann, *Immortality of the Soul or Resurrection of the Dead? The Witness of the New Testament* (London: Epworth Press, 1958), pp. 38f.

26. Cullmann, "The Proleptic Deliverance of the Body According to the New Testament," *The Early Church,* ed. A. J. B. Higgens (London: SCM Press, 1956), pp. 161f.

27. Victor Monod, quoted with approval by Edmund Jacob, *Theology of the Old Testament,* tr. A. W. Heathcote, P. J. Allock (London: Hodder and Stoughton, 1958), p. 149.

28. There can be little doubt that the image of the primeval waters was a common image in the Ancient Near East, and that the Old Testament writers, in this respect as in others, shared the "natural-scientific" views of their time. It seems clear, however, that the image of the world being surrounded by primeval waters *also* had a theological function for the Old Testament writers, namely, to help to indicate how the whole world is totally dependent on the Creator and his continuing activity.

29. Robinson, *op. cit.,* p. 38.

30. On Jesus' "mistake", cf. Werner Georg Kümmel, *Promise and Fulfilment: The Eschatological Message of Jesus,* tr. Dorthea M. Barton (Naperville, Illinois: Alec R. Allenson, 1957), pp. 149-151.

31. Oscar Cullmann, *Christology of the New Testament,* tr. Shirley C. Guthrie, Charles A. M. Hall (Philadelphia: Westminster Press, 1959), p. 224.

32. Cf. *ibid.,* p. 228: "Only in one respect must a limitation be made. Although Christ's Lordship knows no boundaries, its realm nevertheless does not simply coincide with the realm of creation." This idea is developed *loc cit.*

33. For Marcion, it is interesting to note (one would presume this to be the case for all gnostic or quasi-gnostic writers), nature was immutable; cf. Robert M. Grant, *Miracle and Natural Law in Graeco-Roman and Early Christian Thought* (Amsterdam: North Holland Publishing Company, 1952), who cites Harnack. This shows Marcion's distance not only from the Old Testament, but from the New Testament as well. It was only consistent, then, for Marcion to strike out Ro. 8:19ff. From his edition of the New Testament; cf. H. M. Biedermann, *Die Erlösung der Schöpfung beim Apostel Paulus: Ein Beitrag zur Klärung der religionsgeschichtlichen Stellung der paulinischen Erlösungslehre* (Wurzburg: Rita-Verlag, 1940), p. 92.

34. S. R. Driver, *op. cit.,* p. 5: "It [God creating by the Word] is an indication not only of the ease with which He accomplished His work,

and of His omnipotence, but also of the fact that he works consciously and deliberately. Things do not emanate from Him unconsciously, nor are they produced by a mere act of thought, as in some pantheistic systems, but by an act of *will,* of which the concrete word is the outward expression. Each stage of the creation is the realization of a deliberately formed purpose, the 'word' being the mediating principle of creation, the means or agency through which his will takes effect."

35. Jacob, *op. cit.,* p. 136n.
36. *Ibid.,* p. 147.
37. Cf. Robinson, *op. cit.,* p. 8.
38. Jacob, *op cit.,* p. 136n.

CHAPTER FIVE

1. This, for example, is the consistent teaching of Karl Barth. See my dissertation, *Creation and Nature: A Study of the Doctrine of Nature with Special Attention to Karl Barth's Doctrine of Creation,* Harvard University, 1966.

2. It is curious that Paul Tillich, who decisively rejects the idea of Divine personality as such, also gives a pivotal place in his theology to the image the Kingdom of God (see his *Systematic Theology,* III, ii: "History and the Kingdom of God" [Chicago: University of Chicago Press, 1963]). Even employed in the most symbolic way, the metaphor of the Divine Kingdom seems to entail the image of a Divine King, that is, a person who deliberates, acts, responds, loves, etc. It is noteworthy, at the same time, that Tillich was very much aware of the pervasive personalism of biblical thinking (see his *Biblical Religion and the Search for Ultimate Reality* [Chicago: University of Chicago Press, 1955]).

3. The literature on the "Kingdom of God" as a biblical and traditional theological theme is extensive. Only a selection can be cited here. For the Old Testament: Bright, *op. cit.;* Gerhard von Rad, "Basileia," *op. cit.* For the New Testament: Hans Conzelmann, "Reich Gottes: Im NT," *Die Religion in Geschichte und Gegenwart*(3), pp. 914-918; Gösta Lundström, *The Kingdom of God in the Teaching of Jesus: A History of Interpretation from the Last Decades of the Nineteenth Century to the Present Day,* tr. Joan Bulman (Edinburgh: Oliver and Boyd, 1963); Norman Perrin, *The Kingdom of God in the Teaching of Jesus* (Philadelphia: Westminster Press, 1963); Karl Ludwig Schmidt, "Basileia," *Bible Key Words,* II, tr. J. R. Coates, H. P. Kingdon (New York: Harper and Brothers, 1958). Much of the vast literature on the Kingdom of God in the New Testament is cited at various points by the foregoing four writers.

For the history of theology: Johannes Weiss, *Die Idee des Reich Gottes in der Theologie* (Giessen: J. Ricker'sche Verlagsbuchhandlung, 1901), a brief but detailed historical survey from the New Testament to 1900. Ernst Kinder, "Reich Gottes und Kirche bei Augustin," *Luthertum,* XIV (1954). Franz Lau, "Luthers Lehre von dem beiden Reichen," *Luthertum,* VIII(1953). Karfried Fröhlich, *Gottesreich, Welt, und Kirche bei Calvin* (München: Ernst Reinhardt, 1930). Gottlob Schrenk, *Gottesreich und Bund im älteren Protestantismus, vornehmlich bei Johannes Coccejus* (Gütersloh: C. Bertelsmann, 1923). Christian Walther, *Typen des Reich-Gottes-Verständnis: Studien zur Eschatologie und Ethik im 19, Jahrhundert* (München: Christian Kaiser, 1961); single chapters on Kant, Fichte, Hegel, Schleiermacher, Rothe, and Ritschl. The books by Lundström and Perrin also contain material regarding the history of theology, especially in the first half of the twentieth century.

4. Immanuel Kant, *Religion within the Limits of Reason Alone,* tr. Theodore M. Greene, Hoyt H. Hudson (New York: Harper and Row, 1960), book III.

5. Cf. Kinder, *op. cit.,* p. 14: "Die Kirche ist das Reich Gottes in seiner verborgenen Anbahnung, und sie weist hin und führt hin zu dem Reich Gottes in seiner offenbaren Vollendung." "In der Kirche vollzieht sich die legitime Fortsetzung und geschichtliche Manifestierung der Motive der Botschaft Jesu vom Reich Gottes und nicht in der politischen Geschichte oder in kosmischen Ereignissen."

6. Cf. Rev. 1:5b f.: "To him who loves us and has freed us from our sins by his blood and made us a kingdom, priests to his God and Father."

7. He can plan, for example, whether roads should be built through the whole kingdom; whether forest reserves should be set aside; whether certain animals should be given special care; or whether new species of animals and plants should be imported into his kingdom.

8. For example, a newly imported species of tree may not grow in the kingdom; or new and unexpected plants may spring up along the way cleared for a road.

9. Cf. Luther, *WA* 46:559, "Der Vater ist ein solcher, Schöpfer, der, nach dem er angefangen hat alle Ding zu schaffen, noch für und für wirket, sein geschöpf regiert und erhält, also auch ich. Denn täglich sehen wir vor Augen, dass neue Menschen, junge Kinder zur Welt geboren werden, die vor nichts gewesen sind, neue Bäume, neue Tiere auf Erden, neue Fische im Wasser und neue Vögel in der Luft werden, und höret nicht auf zu schaffen und zu nähren bis an den Jungsten Tag." (cited in part by Althaus, *Die Theologie Martin Luthers,* p. 99.) See also Franz Lau, *op. cit.,* pp. 35ff.

10. Cf. Calvin, *Inst* 1. 16. 3.

11. This is also the case in the context of theological epistemology. As Langdon Gilkey remarks concerning the various Christian doctrines, "These are not doctrines about a being called God, but doctrines about the creaturely as the sacred manifests itself in and through the creaturely" (*op. cit.,* p. 466). From the perspective of Christian theology, one does not *know* any other God but the God who has a realm, nor any other realm but the realm which has a God.

CHAPTER SIX

1. See von Rad, *Genesis,* on 2:2f.

2. Teilhard's published writings depict an overwhelmingly, if not totally, *spiritual* consummation of the universe, not also a universal material consummation: "When all else has passed away, concentrated or dispersed, spirit will still remain." (quoted by Emile Rideau, *The Thought of Teilhard de Chardin,* tr. René Hague [New York: Harper and Row, 1967], p. 569, n. 183.) "Is it not conceivable that Mankind, at the end of its totalization, its folding-in upon itself, may reach a critical level of maturity where, leaving Earth and stars to lapse slowly back into the dwindling mass of primordial energy, it will detach itself from this planet and join the one, true, irreversible essence of things, the Omega point?" (Teilhard, *The Future of Man,* tr. N. Denny [New York: Harper and Row, 1964], pp. 122f.) "The end of the world: the wholesale internal introversion upon itself of the noosphere, which has simultaneously reached the uttermost limits of its complexity and its centrality. The end of the world: the overthrow of equilibrium, detaching the mind, fulfilled at last, from its material matrix, so that it will henceforth rest with all its weight in God-Omega." (Teilhard, *The Phenomenon of Man,* tr. B. Wall [New York: Harper Torchbook, 1965], pp. 287f.) Cf. Rideau, *op. cit.,* p. 187: "Thus the 'divinization of the cosmos' [for Teilhard] should be taken as applying to matter only in so far as matter has an integral share in the progress of the spiritual communion of minds, in particular through technical transformations."

3. Irenaeus, *Against Heresies* 5. 36. 1. Cf. Luther, "Psalms III, *Luther's Works,* ed. Jaroslav Pelikan (Saint Louis: Concordia Publishing House, 1958), p. 187: "Just as the heavens will not endure, much less the earth. Hence all creatures will be changed. They will not pass away and perish; they will be renewed."

4. A discussion of the role of evil and death in the created order will be found below in Chapter VI.

5. Bertrand Russell, *Religion and Science* (New York: Henry Holt and Company, 1935), p. 203.

6. Charles Hartshorne, *The Divine Relativity* (New Haven: Yale University Press, 1948).

7. This seems to be the most adequate way of interpreting Acts 1:7, which says that the Father has "fixed" the times and seasons "by his own authority." This is a dynamic, personalistic statement, that God will do what he wants as he wants to do it. It is not a mechanical, authoritarian statement, that everything has been fixed in an unalterable chain of cause and effects for all time. The latter motif, admittedly, does tend to dominate apocalyptic writings; but the dominant theme in Acts 1:7 should be called prophetic rather than apocalyptic. For an elucidation of this distinction, see Perrin, *op. cit.,* pp. 162-185.

8. Charles Hartshorne, *Reality as a Social Process* (Boston: Beacon Press, 1953), p. 161: "Anticipation *grades* possibilities, so that action can take account of the most probable lines of action, and try to bring about the one that is most desirable." "Even God's anticipation would have references to action as choice among probabilities. He would not see what 'is to happen,' but the range of possible things among which what happens will be a selection. And he will see that a higher percentage of some things will happen than others, that is, he will see in terms of probabilities."

9. The spontaneity of nature is discussed in Chapter VIII.

10. On the general idea of God as fountain, cf. the following: Ps. 36:9, "With thee is the fountain of life"; Jer. 2:13, 17:13: God is the "fountain of living waters"; also Rev. 7:17, 21:6. Irenaeus, *op. cit.,* 2. 13. 3: God is "totus fons omnium bonorum"; Augustine, *Confessions,* XIII, iv: God is a "fons vitae"; Calvin, *Inst* 1. 13. 18: "To the Father is attributed the beginning of activity, and the fountain and well-spring of all things"; Westminster Confession (1647), II, ii: "Is omnis entitatis fons est unicus, a quo, per quem et ad quem omnia. . . ." Jonathan Edwards, *Dissertation Concerning the End for which God Created the World,* in *Works,* VI (Worcester, 1809) p. 49: God is referred to as the "author and head of the whole system, on whom all absolutely depend; who is the fountain of being and good for the whole."

11. Luther, *WA* 10:143 (on Heb. 1:3).

12. Calvin, *Inst* 1. 16. 5.

13. *Ibid.* 1. 16. 4, 1.

14. Luther, "Lectures on the Epistle to the Hebrews," *Library of Christian Classics,* ed. and tr. James Atkinson (Philadelphia: Westminster Press, 1962), p. 33.

15. We touch here on the problem of differentiating or identifying creation and providence; we can cautiously pass it by as long as we remain aware that it has not been explicitly resolved. For one resolution, see Friedrich Schleiermacher, *The Christian Faith,* ed. H. R. Mackintosch,

J. S. Stewart (Edinburgh: T. and T. Clark, 1960), section I; for a different resolution, see Barth, *CD* III, iii.

16. Luther, *WA* 18:710.

17. Lest these considerations be misunderstood, we should pause for a moment to consider the theological meaning of "laws of nature." Since both the mind of man and the being and becoming of nature are established by the creative rule of God, and since (as we will see presently) the creative rule of God also orders all things, the "laws of nature" which natural scientists talk about can be said to trace *vestigia* of the creative rule of God; this, whether or not the person doing the tracing recognizes that the order he discerns stems from God.

On the general topic, "laws of nature," see Ernst Troeltsch, "Contingency," *Encyclopedia of Religion and Ethics,* ed. James Hastings (New York: Charles Scribner's Sons, 1902), *s.v.;* Richard R. Niebuhr, *op. cit.,* pp. 165-167; E. L. Mascall, *Christian Theology and Natural Science* (London: Longmans, Green, and Company, 1956), especially p. 89.

In contemporary natural scientific and philosophical reflection about laws of nature and scientific hypotheses, the general tendency seems to be to shy away from the popular idea that laws of nature are immanent forces which *move* nature. Rather, it is generally thought that laws of nature are intra-subjective descriptions of natural occurrences which help us to order our experience and pave the way for further research. Cf. E. F. Caldin, *The Power and Limits of Science* (London: Chapman and Hall, 1949); William G. Pollard, *Chance and Providence: God's Action in a World Governed by Scientific Law* (New York: Charles Scribner's Sons, 1958), p. 60; Philipp Frank, *Philosophy of Science* (Englewood Cliffs, New Jersey: Prentice Hall, 1957), p. 23: "There is no distinction between a principle and a hypothesis. When we begin to take an hypothesis seriously, we call it a principle." Moritz Schlick, *Philosophy of Nature,* tr. Amethe van Zeppelin, ed. Walter Hollitscher (New York: Philosophical Library, 1949), pp. 20f.: "The explanation of nature means a description of nature by means of laws. The function of laws (the meaning of laws) is to *de*-scribe and not to *pre*-scribe." "And when necessity is ascribed to the laws of nature, this means that they are universally valid, and not that they exert force. The laws of a country or state, are forms of compulsion for the citizens of that state. But to speak of compulsion or force, in the case of laws of nature is absurd. One is misled into doing so, because of the ambiguity of the word 'law'—and this, in turn, is due to the half-conscious use of a psychological model."

If one surveys both the theological position taken in this study—that natural laws are descriptions of the works of God in nature—and the growing consensus among natural scientists concerning the same subject, one can speak of a certain convergence of viewpoints.

18. One further clarification can be added here: the creative rule of God should never be viewed alongside of, or in the midst of, what the natural scientists conceive of as natural causality. That would be a *metabasis eis allo genos.* Insofar as the analogy of natural causality can be applied to the Divine rule, it is *the* cause which is in, with, under, and throughout all other causes.

19. Martin Luther, "The Sacrament of the Body and Blood of Christ—Against the Fanatics," *Luther's Works,* ed. Helmut Lehmann, XXXVI, p. 338. Cf. Calvin, *Inst* 1. 14. 21: "For there are as many miracles of divine power, as many tokens of goodness, and as many proofs of wisdom, as there are things in the universe, indeed, as there are things great or small." And Schleiermacher, *On Religion: Speeches to its Cultured Despisers,* tr. John Oman (New York: Harper and Brothers, 1958), p. 88: "Miracle is simply the religious name for event. Every event, even the most natural and usual, becomes a miracle, as soon as the religious view of it can be dominant. To me all is miracle."

20. Augustine, "On the Holy Trinity," in *A Select Library,* III; bk. III, chap. iv, par. 9.

21. See Thomas, *Compendium Theologiae,* I, cxxiv, cxxv. It is true that Thomas holds that no agent can move except by the power of God, and that God is thereby directly the cause of all motion (*Ibid.,* I, cxxx, cxxxi). But this idea of the directness of the Divine power does not materially affect the idea that the same power is mediated more in some instances than in others.

22. John A. Hardon, "The Concept of Miracle from St. Augustine to Modern Apologetics," *Theological Studies,* XV (1954), p. 243. See also T. A. Lacey, *Nature, Miracle and Sin: A Study of St. Augustine's Conception of the Natural Order* (London: Longmans, Green and Company, 1916).

23. Martin Luther, "That These Words of Christ. . . ," *Luther's Works,* ed. Helmut Lehmann, XXXVII, pp. 57f. Italics mine.

24. Calvin, *Inst* 1. 16. 3.

25. On this basis a conception of wondrous events which also offer *salvation* can fittingly be constructed. In chapter IX, for example, we will consider the presence of the Resurrected Christ in the created world as an *extension* of the wondrous working of God throughout the whole creation, an extension of amazing proportions.

26. Von Rad, *Genesis,* p. 58.

27. The First Letter of Clement, 20:1-12.

28. Cf. also Calvin *Inst* 1. 14. 20: ". . . that in a wonderful series he distinguished an innumerable variety of things, that he endowed each kind with its own nature, assigned functions, appointed places and stations."

29. Hugo Rahner, *Man at Play* tr. Brian Battershaw and Edward Quinn (New York: Herder and Herder, 1967), pp. 20, 23.

30. Cf. the interesting remark by the philosopher, Max Scheler, *Man's Place in Nature,* tr. Hans Meyerhoff (Boston: Beacon Press, 1961), p. 13: "The rich variety of forms in the leafy parts of plants suggests even more than the forms and colors in animals, that the principle at the unknown roots of life may act in accordance with fanciful play, regulated by aesthetic order."

31. Martin Luther, "Lectures on Genesis, 1-5" in *Luther's Works,* I, ed. Jaroslav Pelikan (Saint Louis: Concordia Publishing House, 1955), p. 167; cf. Calvin, *Inst* 1. 5. 2.

32. Inst., 1. 5. 1.

33. Cf. the quotations cited by Reinhold Niebuhr, *op. cit.,* I, p. 176.

34. Niebuhr's argument is mainly, though not exclusively, exegetical; see the following note. Althaus argues ("Die Gestalt dieser Welt und die Sünde," *Zeitschrift für systematische Theologie,* IX [1932], pp. 319-338) that the fundamental stance of man "before the fall," that is, man qua created, is fiducial: created man, like redeemed man, must live by every Word from the mouth of God and cannot walk in self-evident certainty (sight) concerning his final state and concerning his life in the future generally. Anxiety, Althaus argues—here picking up a refrain from Kierkegaard which Reinhold Niebuhr (*op. cit.,* I, p. 182) also employs—is as much an aspect of created existence as is joy and peace before God. The presence of physical death and suffering in the world, then, is according to Althaus in a certain sense a necessary concomitant of man's fiducial (faith, not sight) existence. Barth takes a similar position regarding death (*CD* III, ii, p. 632), developing the idea of the "second death" which is mentioned in the Book of Revelation.

35. The idea that physical death results from sin is not taught in the Bible with the unanimity which is often supposed in the theological tradition. As Reinhold Niebuhr has pointed out (*op. cit.,* I, p. 174), the Genesis account (3:17-19) assumes the mortality of man and does not include it as part of the curse. Moreover, as Niebuhr explains, "it is not at all clear that St. Paul consistently regards physical death as the consequence of sin. At any rate he frequently uses the concept of death symbolically to designate spiritual death. . . . Furthermore his classical assertion that the 'sting of death is sin' (I Cor. 15:56) can hardly be interpreted to mean that mortality as such is the consequence of sin. On the contrary, it seems to be in complete accord with the general biblical view of the relation of sin to mortality. In this view mortality, insecurity and dependence are not of themselves evil but become the occasion of evil when man seeks in his pride to hide his mortality, to

overcome his insecurity by his own power and to establish his independence. The ideal possibility would be that a man of perfect faith should not fear death because of his confidence that neither life nor death . . . shall be able to separate us from the love of God which is in Christ Jesus our Lord. But since unbelief is the very basis of sin, it is impossible for sinful man to anticipate his end with equanimity. Thus sin is the 'sting of death'; and the obvious mark of that sting is fear." (*Ibid.*) Niebuhr believes that Paul *also* taught that physical death results from sin, and he cites Romans 5:12. With this text in mind Niebuhr then comments, "It can hardly be denied that the Pauline authority, supporting the idea that physical death is a consequence of sin, introduced a note into Christian theology which is not fully in accord with the total Biblical view of the finiteness of man." (*Ibid.* I, p. 176)

36. See Appendix.

37. Cf. Emil Brunner's instructive formulation, *Man in Revolt,* tr. Olive Wyon (Philadelphia: Westminster Press, 1939), p. 318: Not *principium individuationis est materia,"* but *"principium individuationis est voluntas Dei Creatoris."*

38. Perhaps it will not be out of place here to cite an instance of the shaping moment of the creative rule of God which is somewhat more homely than the snowflake. In commenting on Aristotle's suggestion that mice emerge from decaying matter, Luther writes ("Lectures on Genesis," p. 52): "The sun warms; but it would bring nothing into being unless God said by his divine power: 'let a mouse come out of the decay.' Therefore the mouse, too, is a divine creature . . . for its kind it has a very beautiful form—such pretty feet and such delicate hair that it is clear that it was created by the Word of God with a definite plan in view. Therefore we should admire God's creation and workmanship. The same thing may be said about flies."

39. The God depicted in the Bible not only calls men by name (cf. Jn. 10:3), he also calls the stars and planets by name (Is. 40:26f; Ps. 147:7; Job 38:37). Not a sparrow falls without his notice and even the hairs on our heads are numbered (cf. Lk. 12:6f.).

40. Muir, *1000 Mile Walk,* p. 377.

41. See H. Richard Niebuhr's essay, "Center of Value," in *Radical Monotheism and Western Culture* (New York: Harper and Brothers, 1943), pp. 100-114, for an astute discussion of the complex of problems we are touching on here.

42. Barth, *CD* III, i, p. 62; italics added; the translation is mine.

43. Cf. Luther's comment on Heb. 1:3, concerning the Word *upholding* all things, "Lectures on the Epistle to the Hebrews," p. 33: "This word captures the idea of a certain delightful care in cherishing the

things he created, even a motherly care we might say. The idea is found in Dt. 32:11, " 'He spread out his wings and took him up, and carried him on his back.' "

44. Edwards, *op. cit.,* p. 10.

45. This is clear both from the Genesis creation narratives and from the theme that God gives man dominion over nature. This also is the teaching apparently the unanimous teaching—of the whole theological tradition: that nature is posited and shaped by God for the sake of man. In an otherwise edifying book, Richard H. Overman has veered away from this biblical and traditional theological motif (*Evolution and the Christian Doctrine of Creation: A Whiteheadian Interpretation* [Philadelphia: Westminster Press, 1967]). He writes: "The evolution of man was but one way in which the divine aim for the beauty of creaturely experience might reach concrete expression." "It may be that as God envisioned the future a billion years ago, he was quite indifferent as to whether *homo sapiens* would turn out to be the avenue through which his aims for beauty on earth are now mainly channeled." (p. 289) As a reaction to the anthropocentrism of mainstream modern theology's approach to nature, Overman's viewpoint is understandable. But it can hardly be justified theologically.

46. Cf. Luther, "Lectures on Genesis," p. 42: "Night and day alternate for the purposes of refreshing our bodies by rest. The sun shines that work may be done." And Calvin, *Inst* 1. 14. 22: "before he fashioned man, [God] prepared everything he foresaw would be useful and salutary to him."

CHAPTER SEVEN

1. Barth, *CD,* III, iii, pp. 132, 135. In his study *Issues in Science and Religion* (Englewood Cliffs, New Jersey; Prentice Hall, 1966), p. 424, Ian Barbour has criticized Barth for not explaining *how* human freedom and natural causation are related to the creative work of God. Barbour attempts to do this, following Whitehead, by projecting the idea of a self-limitation on the part of God, which allows the created world a certain autonomy. "God's activity," Barbour explains, "is thus more akin to *persuasion* that to compulsion. He does not determine the outcome of events or violate the self-creation of all beings; he is never the sole cause, but one influence among others." (p. 442) At the same time, however, Barbour has certain important reservations about the Whiteheadian conception of a persuading Deity, reservations which seem to undercut much, if not all, of the force of the conception. Barbour notes that in the Whiteheadian representation "God lacks both the sovereign control and the moral intensity of the biblical Jehovah." And Barbour

adds, "God's ability to engender creative change in lower beings seems to be very limited [according to the Whiteheadian conceptualization]. But even in the case of man, one wonders whether Whitehead's God is *too powerless* to inspire worship. Perhaps in addition to the 'persuasive' aspects of God there are more active and authoritative aspects, to which the sense of inescapable and overwhelming awe in religious experience testify." (p. 448) Is not the root problem here Barbour's dissatisfaction with any cognitive tension in theological discourse? Would not his problem with Whitehead be much less severe if, with Barth, Barbour were prepared to admit a certain lack of understanding here, rather than trying to bring every aspect of the God-world relationship under the rule of human conceptuality? This is not to suggest that paradox should be a goal in theological reasoning; it is to suggest, however, that paradox ought to be anticipated and accepted, at least in the initial stages of theological reflection, lest we lose sight of important theological motifs. Barbour himself quotes Niels Bohr, whose words seem relevant in this regard: "A complete elucidation of one and the same object may require diverse points of view which defy a unique description."

2. The analogy of the river is chosen here mainly because it seems to be a suitable concomitant for the analogy of the creative Divine rule as the immediate and continuing source of all things. The analogy of the river also commends itself because in the Old Testament the image of primeval waters is used to suggest the state of creation at the very foundation, of creation, where God alone has power to keep creation from becoming a chaos (cf. Gen. 1:2, Ps. 29:3, 93:1-3).

3. It is conceivable that the Psalmists and the Old Testament generally presuppose some kind of pan-psychic world-view, for example, when nature is called upon to praise God. But this is by no means self-evident. Indeed the Old Testament writers do not show any direct interest in pan-psychism. At one place, at least, pan-psychism seems to be expressly denied, in Psalm 19:1ff. More generally, one would expect to meet a turning away from pan-psychism in the Old Testament, given pan-psychism's proximity to animism and, close to that, polytheism. One can read the Priestly creation narrative, for example, as a demythologizing and a desacralizing of nature. Yahweh the creator, not independent creaturely souls in rocks and trees is the chief Old Testament interest in this regard.

4. Calvin has a similar, if implicit, notion of the spontaneity and continuity of nature in relationship to the rule of God. His view is worth recalling here at length. At one point he writes this regarding the history of creation in Genesis 1 and 2(*Inst* 1. 14. 20): "From this history we shall learn that God by the power of his Word and Spirit created heaven and earth out of nothing: that thereupon he brought forth

living beings and inanimate things of every kind, that he endowed each kind with its own nature, assigned functions, appointed places and stations; and that, although all were subject to corruption, he nevertheless provided for the preservation of each species until the Last Day. We shall likewise learn that he nourishes some in secret ways, and, as it were, from time to time instills new vigor into them; on others he has conferred the power of propagating, lest by their death entire species perish; that he has so wonderfully adorned heaven and earth with as unlimited abundance, variety, and beauty of all things as could possibly be, quite like a spacious and splendid house, provided and filled with the most exquisite and at the same time the most abundant furnishings." Most of what Calvin says can be affirmed here, except his outdated notion that all species were present at the very beginning and will be present at the very end.

5. Barth, *CD,* III, ii, p. 426.

6. In the Old Testament a distinction is made between the body, *basar,* and the soul, *nephesh.* But the "*nephesh* is not a spiritual entity which enters the body at birth and leaves it as such at death; it is simply a principle of life which makes the body effective, and the body is the real basis of personality." (Robinson, *op. cit.,* p. 70) In a certain sense the *nephesh* is more than the body; but the body is always thought to be a perfectly valid manifestation of the *nephesh* (Johannes Pedersen, *Israel: Its Life and Culture,* I-II, tr. A. Møller [London: Oxford University Press, 1963], p. 171.) Moreover, the Old Testament never hints at any contrast between a weak flesh and a strong soul. (*Ibid.,* p. 176) Accordingly, the "image of God" is conceived of as referring to the whole man, body and soul. Indeed, the idea of bodily resemblance even seems to predominate: "Man is a representative by his entire being, for Israelite thought always views man in his totality, by his physical being as well as by his spiritual functions, and if the choice had to be made between the two we would say that the external appearance is perhaps even more important than the spiritual resemblance." (Jacob, *op. cit.,* p. 168)

Paul may be taken as an exponent of a generally accepted New Testament view of body and soul. Paul is much influenced by the Old Testament view of man as psycho-somatic unity. He has no idea of the soul being better than the body; on the contrary it is the *sōma psuxikon* that is inferior, and *psuxikos* is almost always used in a bad sense. (M. E. Dahl, *The Resurrection of the Body: A Study of I Corinthians 15* [London: SCM Press, 1962], p. 56) The contrast in Paul's thought is not between body and soul, but between man as *sarx* and man as *sōma*: "While *sarx* stands for man, in the solidarity of creation, in his distance from God, *sōma* stands for man, in the solidarity of creation, as made for God." (John A. T. Robinson, *The Body: A Study in Pauline Theology* [London: SCM Press, 1957], p. 31). Moreover, *sarx* and *sōma* cannot be contrasted in terms of their constituents; *sarx* can include mental functions and *sōma* includes man's physical being (*ibid.*, p. 31n.)

7. It is true that Paul talks about a spiritual body replacing the physical body on the Day of Resurrection (I Cor. 15:44ff.). But, for Paul, *sōma* refers to the entire person (see preceding note), so that pericope is not relevant to the question whether the *soul* can take on a new body. Paul is referring to the radical change which the *whole person* will undergo on the Final Day. A text which *is* relevant to the question before us is found outside the New Testament canon, in the Apostolic Creed. And here we are left in no doubt concerning the question whether our souls will take on new bodies at the time of the Resurrection: there will be a resurrection of the flesh (*resurrectio carnis*). The New Testament witness to the Empty Tomb also suggests similar implications, as does the Johannine text dealing with Thomas and the resurrected Christ (Jn. 20:27).

8. Immanuel Kant, *Critique of Pure Reason,* tr. Norman Kemp Smith (London: Macmillan and Company, 1958), A 550, B 578.

9. Reinhold Niebuhr, *Nature and Destiny of Man,* I, p. 40.

10. Cf. *ibid.*, II, p. 296: "Climate and geographic limits, poverty and plenty, the survival impulse and sexual desires, and all natural conditions leave their indelible mark upon the spiritual constructions of history. Yet historical achievements transcend these limits in varying degrees of freedom." Also, Reinhold Niebuhr, *The Self and the Dramas of History* (New York: Charles Scribner's Sons, 1955), p. 23: "There can be no question, of course, that the self is an object among other objects in space and time. It has its dated existence at some particular location. The conditions of time and space, of age and environment determine its character to a large degree. But the self also rises indubitably out of the situation of time and place. The self, Niebuhr explains, is both in space and time and beyond them; "and there is no sharp distinction between its spatial and non-spatial dimensions." (*op. cit.*, p. 24)

11. Cf. the interesting observation by Mumford, *op. cit.,* p. 128f., concerning the introduction of the mirror into the Western world: "Glass had a profound effect upon the development of personality; indeed it helped to alter the very concept of the self." Mumford relates the introduction of the mirror in the Western world to the rise of the introspective biography. Elsewhere (*op. cit.,* p. 243) he relates the introduction of the camera to the rise of behavioristic sociology and psychology. Also, René Dubos, *So Human An Animal* (New York: Charles Scribner's Sons, 1968), p. 18: ". . . in other words, anatomic structures and physical performance, as well as behavioral patterns, are

molded by the surroundings and the conditions of life during childhood; furthermore, the effects of such early influences commonly persist throughout the whole life span. For example, a child brought up in Florence is constantly exposed to the sights, sounds, and smells characteristic of this beautiful city. . . . He may not be aware of the responses aroused in him by these repeated experiences. But they become part of his biological make-up and render him lastingly different from what he would have become had he developed in London, Paris, or New York."

12. Cf. again, Dubos, *op. cit.,* p. 17: "Contrary to popular belief, genes do not determine the traits of a person; they merely govern his responses to the physical and social environment. Furthermore, not all the genes of a person are active at all times. Through complex mechanisms that are only now being recognized, environmental stimuli determine which parts of the genetic equipment are repressed and which parts are activated. Thus each individual person is as much the product of the environment as of his genetic development. Human beings perceive the world, and respond to it, not through the whole spectrum of their potentialities, but only through the areas of the spectrum that have been made functional by environmental stimulation. The life experiences determine what parts of the genetic endowment are converted into functional attributes."

13. Note the following remark concerning the Franciscan approach to nature: "The Franciscan was conscious of Nature, not so much as something outside and apart from himself, but rather as the world in which he had his being: it entered intimately into his very consciousness of himself: it was, so to speak, his larger self, much in the same way as the patriot regards his country." (F. Cuthbert, *The Romanticism of St. Francis and Other Studies in the Genius of the Franciscans,* 2nd ed. [London: Longmans, Green, and Company, 1924], p. 49).

14. In the Bible God is depicted as speaking his Word to nature, but nature is not depicted as responding self-consciously to this Word, whereas man does respond in this way.

15. Cf. Reinhold Niebuhr, *Nature and Destiny of Man,* I, p. 55: "Man, unlike animal existence, not only has a centre, but he has a centre beyond himself. Man is the only animal which can make itself its own object."

16. Cf. Luther, "Lectures on Genesis," p. 68: "The rest of the animals are designated as footprints of God; but man alone is God's image, as appears in the *Sentences.* . . . In the human being, especially in Adam, He is truly recognized, because in him there is such wisdom, justice, and knowledge of all things that he may rightly be called a world in miniature."

17. On the idea of man imitating God, see Eph. 4:17-5:2.

18. Although at first this point may seem to tie the hands of the natural scientist, were he to accept it, actually when it is taken in conjunction with the idea of man's Divinely granted dominion, it has the opposite effect. Whereas the idea of man's dominion gives hope for real understanding of nature, the idea of nature's mystery encourages us not to be satisfied with any one complex of ideas about nature (for example, Newtonian physics), but to search for more and more understanding.

19. A special problem arises concerning whether man may rightfully kill those animals which closely resemble man himself (as distinct from one-celled animals, insects, etc.). Karl Barth has drawn attention to a "marked silence" concerning man eating the meat of animals (Gen. 1:30) in the Book of Genesis(Barth, *CD* KD, III, iv, p. 353) It is not until the Noah story (9:2f.) that man is explicitly given the animals for food. The suggestion being made here is that animals can be rightfully killed by man, and that this is not a mere providential adjustment on the part of God to a sinful world. This point, admittedly, stands in tension with the Priestly theology of the Old Testament. However, it seems necessary to make the point in order to do full justice to the New Testament understanding of man's value as being more than nature's value.

20. Cf. Dubos, *op. cit.*, p. 19: "One can take it for granted that the latent potentialities of human beings have a better chance to become actualized when the social environment is sufficiently diversified to provide a variety of stimulating experiences, especially for the young. As more persons find the opportunity to express their biological endowment under diversified conditions, society becomes richer in experiences and civilizations continue to unfold. In contrast, if the surroundings and ways of life are highly stereotyped, the only components of man's nature that flourish are those adapted to the narrow range of prevailing conditions."

21. See my article, "I-Thou, I-It, and I-Ens," *Journal of Religion*, XLVII, 3 (July 1968), pp. 260-273.

22. The discussion that follows is patterned after Martin Buber's description of the I-Thou relation, *mutatis mutandis* (*I and Thou*, tr. Ronald G. Smith [New York: Charles Scribner's Sons, 1959]. My objections to Buber's use of the concept I-Thou to describe a relationship to a *tree* are outlined in the article cited in the previous note.

23. Buber, *I and Thou*, p. 16.

24. Cf. *ibid.*, p. 16.

25. One immediate ramification of these considerations is the restriction of the primary-secondary qualities distinction to the I-It relation. When one asks what the tree is "really like" apart from human perception and understanding, one has already entered the sphere of the I-It relation.

26. The point here is that the I-Ens relation is characterized by a perduring kind of contemplation which comes to a rest, as it were, in the entity contemplated. A different kind of contemplation is involved in the I-It relation; here one looks at the object with a view as to how it relates to an end or ends outside of the objects as it is presently given. Man as overlord and caretaker always engages himself with the object in order to manipulate it to some extent.

27. Cf. Calvin, *Inst* 1. 14. 21: "While we contemplate in all creatures, as in mirrors, those immense riches of his wisdom, justice, goodness, and power, we should not merely run them over cursorily, and, so to speak, with a fleeting glance; but we should ponder them at length, turn them over in our minds seriously and faithfully, and recollect them repeatedly."

28. It might be said that the progress of natural-scientific knowledge, with its disclosure of the intricate workings of natural entities, inhibits the development and preservation of the I-Ens relation. In a sense this is true. But the creative scientist—as distinguished from the technician—never falls into the trap of believing that he is in perfect control of his material. He senses that nature is much more complex and much more simple than he can imagine, and in this awareness he continually enters into the I-Ens relation. Many natural scientists will gladly acknowledge this to be the case. On the other hand, one can agree with the following observation: "Unfortunately that true sense of the mystery of things which may, in fact, deepen in the course of scientific investigation, and which seems at the root of genuine humility in the investigator, finds no articulate place in the articulated results of scientific investigation." "Thus the wonder, respect, and love for things investigated, which may be at the heart of the scientific experience, virtually escapes reflective interpretation and testimony." (Henry Bugbee, *The Inward Morning: A Philosophical Exploration in Journal Form* [State College, Pennsylvania: Bald Eagle Press, 1958, p. 169].)

29. On the difference between the beautiful and the sublime, see Immanuel Kant, *Critique of Aesthetic Judgment,* tr. James C. Meredith (Oxford: Clarendon Press, 1911), p. 90; E. F. Carritt, *The Theory of Beauty* (London: Methuen and Company, 1914), pp. 241f.

30. Muir, *1000 Mile Walk,* p. 406. As this quotation indicates, the I-Ens relations can obtain between a person and a constellation of natural objects as well as between a person and an individual natural entity. Conceivably, one can even relate oneself to the universe as a whole in an I-Ens relation. Cf. Muir, *Travels in Alaska,* p. 6: "The scenery of the ocean, however sublime in vast expanse, seems far less

beautiful to us dry-shod animals than that of the land seen only in comparatively small patches; but when we contemplate the whole globe as one great dewdrop, striped and dotted with continents and islands, flying through space with other stars all singing and shining together as one, the whole universe appears as an infinite storm of beauty."

31. Calvin, *Commentaries on the First Book of Moses Called Genesis,* I, tr. John King (Edinburgh: Edinburgh Printing Co., 1847), p. 85.

32. Luther, *WA* 19:496.

33. Muir, *1000 Mile Walk,* p. 301.

34. Cf. Muir, *The Mountains of California,* I, 161f.: "Few indeed, strong and free with eyes undimmed with care, have gone far enough and lived long enough with trees to gain anything like a loving conception of their grandeur and significance through the seasons."

35. These moods are respectively concomitant with objects which are sublime and beautiful.

36. Herman Melville, *Moby Dick or the White Whale* (New York: New American Library, 1961), pp. 405, 334, 196.

37. Calvin, *Genesis,* p. 106; *Calvini Opera* 23:22f.; *Inst.* 1. 14. 20.

38. Muir, *Travels in Alaska,* p. 21. Cf. Muir, *Mountains of California,* I, 146f.: "With inexpressible delight you wade out into the grassy sun-lakes, feeling yourself contained in one of Nature's most sacred chambers, withdrawn from the sterner influence of the mountains, secure from all intrusion, secure from yourself, free in universal beauty."

39. This formulation is employed, in part, in order to leave open the question concerning a general *revelation* in the natural world. It could be, in other words, that the sense for the presence of God is not founded on a self-disclosure of God in nature as such, but on a self-disclosure of God in some other way (for example, through the preached Word), the experience of which is somehow reenacted by the subject in his encounter with the Ens.

40. Calvin, *CO* 38:59, cited and tr. by Brunner, *Revelation and Reason,* p. 68n.; also, *Genesis,* p. 57.

41. Cf. Schleiermacher, *Speeches,* p. 87: "Every finite thing, however, is a sign of the Infinite, and so these various expressions declare the immediate relation of a phenomenon to the Infinite and the Whole."

42. Muir, *Our National Parks,* p. 328; and *Travels in Alaska,* p. 84. Cf. Muir, *Mountains of California,* I, pp. 196f.: "In the morning everything is joyous and bright, the delicious purple of the dawn changes softly to daffodil yellow and white. . . . The birds begin to stir. . . . Innumerable insects begin to dance, the deer withdraw from the open glades and ridge tops. . . . the flowers open and straighten their petals as the dew

vanishes, every pulse beats high, every life cell rejoices, the very rocks seem to tingle with life, and God is felt brooding over everything great and small."

43. Philipp Melanchthon, "Enarr. Symb. Nic.," *Corpus Reformatorum,* 22:239.

44. From a theological perspective, this designation, "brother earth," is much to be preferred over the common parlance "mother earth" (found, among other places, in Francis's Hymn to the Sun). That way of speaking is much too closely tied to the theme Nature versus Civilization to be useful any longer; it suggests that one's major allegiance in life is to nature.

CHAPTER EIGHT

1. For a lengthy discussion of Barth's thought, and an attempt to evaluate its christocentrism, see my dissertation, *op. cit.*

2. For a review of Origen's thinking about the fall, see Galloway, *op. cit.,* pp. 85ff.

3. Irenaeus, *op. cit.,* 2. 28. 7.

4. Luther, "Lectures on Genesis," p. 205; Calvin, *Inst* 1. 6. 1.

5. See Appendix.

6. Cf. Ragnar Leivestad, *Christ the Conqueror* (New York: Macmillan, 1954), p. 94, on *ta stoicheia tou kosmou:* "They are not regarded as the passive raw material of which the world was made, but rather as fate-controlling supernatural powers, on whose harmonious cooperation the whole universe is dependent."

7. This is to leave open the question of the relation of man to the demonic. For Paul, for example, sin is not just an evil deed by man; it is a personal satanic power (Anthony Hanson, *The Wrath of the Lamb* (London: S.P.C.K., 1957), p. 61). Still, for Paul sin has its seat in man [see Appendix].

8. Luther, "Lectures on Genesis," p. 66.

9. Whitehead, *Science and the Modern World,* p. 17.

10. Luther, *WA* 42:155f.; italics added. Cf. Pedersen, *op. cit.,* I-II, p. 486: "Thorn and thistles belong in the wilderness, and only through the curse are they made to crop up in the world of man."

11. Calvin, *Inst* 1. 6. 1.

12. Reinhold Niebuhr, *Nature and Destiny of Man,* I, p. 138.

13. William Shakespeare, "King Lear," IV, ii.

14. Aldous Huxley, "Wordsworth in the Tropics," *Collected Essays* (London: Chatto and Windus, 1960).

15. Shakespeare, "As You Like It," II, i,; "A Midsummer Night's Dream," I, i.

16. Luther, "Sermons on the Gospel of John (Chapters 1-4)," *Luther's Works,* XXII, ed. Jaroslav Pelikan (Saint Louis: Concordia Publishing House, 1957), p. 496.

17. Since Galloway, *op. cit.,* accepts the extra-biblical idea of a cosmic fall, he is forced to extend his concept of the cosmic work of Christ to include the notion that Christ works directly on nature in some way. Biblical theology does not permit us to extend the work of Christ to nature in *that* sense, since it does not presuppose a cosmic fall.

18. What "actually happened" to the sea, it seems to me, is a question the text passes by with a sovereign lack of concern. The important point is—Who is this? The answer is, the One who brings peace to the whole world, to man-in-nature as well as man-in-history. Cf. the exegesis of Mark 1:13 ("he was with the wild beasts") by Erich Fascher, *op. cit.:* "Das 'Sein mit den Tieren' ist kein feindliches, auch kein farblesneutral (in Sinne eines Nicht-Bedrohtseins) sondern, wie ander Stellen bei Mk. erwiesen, positiv zu verstehen." "Jesus was mit dem Tieren, aber er war nich mit dem Satan." "Samt sind die Tiere von Mk. 1:13 nicht bloss Staffage für die Wüste, um den Ort des Grauens zu illustrieren. Der Versucher ist nicht bloss um der Menschen willen abgeschlagen, er ist besiegt, um den Frieden im Gottes gesamter Schöpfung wiederherzustellen, so das es keine Feindschaft zwischen Menschen und Tier, Mensch und Engel mehr gibt." (p. 576)

19. John Milton, "On the Morning of Christ's Nativity," "The Hymn," v.

20. Cf. Calvin, *Inst* 1. 6. 1.: "Therefore, since we have fallen from life into death, the whole knowledge of God the Creator that we have discussed would be useless unless faith also followed, setting forth for us God our Father in Christ."

21. Luther, *WA*-TR 1:1160; cited and tr. by Heinrich Bornkamm, *Luther's World of Thought,* tr. Martin H. Bertram (Saint Louis: Concordia Publishing House, 1958), p. 184; also, Luther, "The Gospel According to Saint John (I-LV)," p. 496.

22. Luther, "Lectures on Genesis," p. 67.

23. Gustaf Wingren, *Man and the Incarnation: A Study in the Biblical Theology of Irenaeus,* tr. Ross MacKenzie (Philadelphia: Muhlenberg Press, 1959), p. 25.

24. Oscar Cullmann, *Christ and Time,* tr. Floyd V. Filson (Philadelphia: Westminster Press, 1951).

25. Richard R. Niebuhr, *op. cit.,* p. 177, has made a similar point regarding the Resurrection's relationship to history: "In the Resurrection of Christ, the spontaneity, particularity, and independence of historical events rise to the surface in a single irruption."

26. *Ibid.,* p. 77.

27. Cf. *ibid.,* 178: "But in another sense, conveyed better by the biblical word, *scandal,* the miraculous quality of the resurrection cannot be effaced, for it is an event that cannot be assimilated to the image of death. Our experience of nature and of history, deeply colored by our knowledge of dying and fear of death, openly conflicts with the resurrection of Christ."

28. For one succinct statement of such an approach to worship, see Alexander Schmemann, *For the Life of the World* (New York: National Student Christian Federation, 1963).

29. Cf. Oscar Cullmann, *Immortality of the Soul or Resurrection of the Dead? The Witness of the New Testament* (London: Epworth Press, 1958), p. 45: "Here in communion with the brethren we come nearest to the Resurrection Body of Christ; and so Paul writes in the following chapter 11(a passage which has received far too little consideration): if this Lord's Supper were partaken of by all members of the community in a completely worthy manner, then the union with Jesus's resurrection Body would be so effective in our own bodies that even now there would be no more sickness or death (I Cor. 11:28-30)—a singularly bold assertion."

30. Cf. Cullmann, *op. cit.,* p. 44, speaking of the "foretaste" motif, noting that Paul designates the Holy Spirit by the same term, *aparche,* first-fruits, (Ro. 8:23) as he used for Jesus Himself (I Cor. 15:23): "There is then already a foretaste of the Resurrection. And indeed in a twofold way: our inner man is already being renewed from day to day by the Holy Spirit (II Cor. 4:16, Eph. 3:16); the body also has already been laid hold of by the Spirit, although the flesh still has its citadel within it."

31. Of a communion between Christ and *non*-human creatures now in this world, we simply have no word in the Scriptures. Hence, from a theological perspective, such a notion must be regarded as speculation.

32. Luther, "Psalms, I," pp. 119, 121.

CHAPTER NINE

1. See the unpublished paper by Norman J. Faramelli, "Endless Growth and Eventual Disaster: Links Between Economic Growth, Justice, and Ecological Limits," Boston Industrial Mission, Cambridge, Mass., May, 1970: "Today, the United States with roughly 6% of the world's population consumes around 40-50% of the non-renewable resources utilized each year. According to some estimates, by 1985, the United States will have about 5% of the world's population and will consume around 55-70% of those resources in order to continuously increase its 'standard of living'."

2. Many leap to the conclusion today that every family should have no more than two children (hopefully fewer). Perhaps that replacement quota must eventually become some kind of an axiom. But it sounds like male chauvinism—assuming that all women want to bear children. Would it not therefore be better to work to create the kind of society in which women can regularly find genuine satisfaction in other roles, a society in which women are not compelled by social pressure to desire to be mothers consciously or unconsciously, and then allow women who truly wish to devote their creative efforts to motherhood to plan their families with freedom as well as obligation?

3. This phrase should be remembered. We must avoid that easy romanticism which simplistically assumes that once one has sold one's own goods and given to the poor one has become a disciple of Jesus. That may make a person feel good, but it does little in the long run for the poor. "Giving to the poor" in our present-day American context means responsible participation in the politics of social justice, in addition to even the most radical kind of personal philanthropy.

4. René Dubos, *The Torch of Life: Continuity in Living Experience* (New York: Simon and Schuster, 1962), p. 68.

5. Barbara Delp, Wellesley College, Class of 1973, unpublished poem.

APPENDIX

1. Pedersen, *Israel,* pp. 170, 458, 474, 459.

2. The New Testament differs from the Old in a like manner, it is interesting to observe, with respect to political life. Although the holiness of God is taken as seriously in the New Testament as in the Old, in the former the judgmental activity of God over the political sphere tends to be identified with the coming of the Last Day, whereas in the Old Testament, especially in the prophetic literature, God's judgmental activity over political life is apprehended in contemporary events as well as in the coming of a Last Day.

3. Leivestad, *op. cit.,* p. 95, has noted the general conformity between Paul's statements about the law and his statements about cosmic powers. On the Galation pericope in particular, cf. Bo Reicke, "The Law and This World according to Paul," *Journal of Biblical Literature,* LXX (1951), pp. 259-276.

4. Christ takes away the curse of the law (Gal. 3:13). This is so that the blessing of Abraham might come on the gentiles (Gal. 3:14), which blessing includes the inheritance of the world (Ro. 4:13).

5. As does Cullmann in his excursus on Ro. 13 in *The State in the New Testament* (London: SCM Press, 1957).

6. On Ro. 1:1iff. C. H. Dodd, *The Epistle of Paul to the Romans* (New York: Harper and Brothers, 1932), *loc. cit.*

7. *Ibid.*, p. 37.

8. Leivestad, *op. cit.*, p. 93.

9. On this pericope see the detailed study of Biedermann, *op. cit.* He argues convincingly that Romans 8:19ff. is best viewed against the Old Testament background. Contrast Rudolf Bultmann, *A Theology of the New Testament*, tr. Kendrick Grobel (London: SCM Press, 1955), I, p. 174; Bultmann assumes that this passage stems from Gnostic mythology.

10. N. A. Dahl, "Two Notes on Romans 5," *Studia Theologica,* V (1951), pp. 37-48. Biedermann, *op. cit.,* pp. 88f., independently of Dahl, has made the same suggestion only with more attention to detail.

11. Biedermann, *op. cit.,* p. 74; Lindeskog, *op. cit.,* p. 183.

12. The contrast between this and Gnosticism is striking.

13. On this cf. Biedermann, *op. cit.,* p. 89; Lindeskog, *op. cit.,* p. 183f. and C. K. Barrett, *From First Adam to Last: A Study in Pauline Theology* (New York: Charles Scribners, 1962), p. 117.

14. So Lietzmann, Dibelius (references cited by Biedermann, *op. cit.,* p. 90)

15. F. W. Beare, "Colossians," *Interpreter's Bible,* on Col. 1:15ff.

16. *Ibid.*

17. Brevard S. Childs, *Myth and Reality in the Old Testament* (Naperville, Illinois: Alec R. Allenson, 1960), p. 77.

18. *Ibid.,* chap. IV.

19. Cf. chap. VI, note 35 above.

20. Cf. the remarks on Origen and Irenaeus at the beginning of chap. VIII above.

Index